No. 2728
$15.95

DEMYSTIFYING
COMPACT
DISCS
A GUIDE TO
DIGITAL AUDIO

DANIEL SWEENEY

TAB TAB BOOKS Inc.
Blue Ridge Summit, PA 17214

FIRST EDITION

FIRST PRINTING

Copyright © 1986 by TAB BOOKS Inc.

Printed in the United States of America

Library of Congress Cataloging in Publication Data

Sweeney, Daniel, 1948-
    Demystifying compact discs.

    Includes index.
    1. Compact discs. 2. Sound—Recording and reproducing—Digital techniques. I. Title.
TK7882.C56S94 1986   621.389′3   86-14425
ISBN 0-8306-0628-9
ISBN 0-8306-2728-6 (pbk.)

Cover photographs courtesy of NAD ELECTRONICS, INC.

Contents

Introduction

The compact disc and the compact disc player are the first fundamentally new products to be offered by the audio industry to the consumer in over a quarter of a century. The compact disc is currently revolutionizing consumer audio, and the advent of the compact disc has frequently been likened to the introduction of the stereo phonograph record in 1958 or the 33 1/3 rpm LP in 1948. But the compact disc actually represents a change of far greater magnitude than either. Unlike the LP or the stereo record, it is not a refinement of the traditional analog phonograph first developed by Edison way back in 1878, but an essentially different medium utilizing computer technology.

Thus, it is no surprise that the compact disc is little understood by the public at large in spite of its great success in the marketplace.

Few consumers understand how compact disc players operate or how to use them to their best advantage in a home entertainment system, and fewer still know what criteria to use when assessing individual machines. This book is intended to provide all three kinds of information—a basic laypersons' explanation of operating principles; a guide to incorporating compact disc players in your home system, your automobile or any of several other applications; and the means for determining the worth of individual machines. Also discussed is a related video format called the Laserdisc, and a word about the still-evolving consumer digital audio tape formats and the as yet experimental recordable compact disc.

The reader whose primary interest is in understanding the mechanism and operation of the players may concentrate on Chapters 1 to 4. The reader interested in applications or in secondary digital media may focus on the remainder of the book, Chapters 5 to 8, although the first chapter will provide useful background information for this reader as well.

Chapter 5, the longest chapter in this book, has much to say about audio systems in general and can be read with profit by anyone assembling a component stereo system, whether or not it contains a compact disc player.

This book is intended for the layperson who lacks formal instruction in basic electronics or acoustics. But the compact disc does represent a highly developed technology, and there are limits to the understanding one can gain concerning the medium without some grounding in electronics.

This book is not sponsored by any manufacturer of compact discs or compact disc playback equipment, though several companies have provided me with information, including Luxman, P.S. Audio, Sony, ADS, Denon, and Yamaha. Nor is this book intended to support the idea that compact discs provide for perfect reproduction of sound, a notion that has bulked large in the promotional campaigns launched by several manufacturers on behalf of the new medium. In theory, digital recording offers the potential of lossless recording and transmission of audio information. In practice, digital systems function imperfectly, and the technology of digital recording and reproduction cannot be said to be completely mature.

In this text I will use the term *compact disc* and its abbreviation, *CD*, interchangeably. Both refer to the same entity: a 4 3/4-inch, laser-scanned, laminated disc containing a digital sound track, but ordinarily no video information. This medium is occasionally referred to as a DAD (digital audio disc), but that term appears to be passing into disuse. The Laserdisc in 12-inch and 8-inch sizes is a totally different medium with a video track as well as audio. At least in its initial form, the Laserdisc used an analog audio track, not digital.

Chapter 1

The CD Revolution

In the summer of 1983, a puzzling new audio component began to appear on the shelves of consumer electronics retailers throughout the United States. Called a digital audio disc player, the new gadget had about the same dimensions as an FM tuner or a cassette tape recorder (Fig. 1-1). Instead of tape or phonograph records, it used a small (approximately 4 3/4-inch) plastic disc with a silvery, iridescent surface. The disc rotated within a sealed housing and one never really saw the specifics of operation, but promotional literature indicated that the information on the disc was somehow read by a "laser eye." Everything was push button—cueing, repeat functions, program selection—and only one side of the disc was played. The player was connected via standard RCA connector cables to an ordinary preamplifier or receiver in just the same manner as a cassette deck, but, unlike a cassette deck, it could not record. It was definitely different.

If you chanced to stop and examine the machine and you weren't put off by the $900-plus cost (prices have since come down dramatically), the salesperson would launch into a lengthy explanation of its many virtues—which included perfect reproduction of music, no distortion, 90dB dynamic range (whatever that was), and no noise. "No noise?" some hundreds of thousands of curious people asked when that claim was presented. The salesperson, warming to his task, then put on a phonograph record on an adjacent turntable and a cassette in a waiting cassette deck. Switching be-

Fig. 1-1. The changing of the guard—Shure D5000 compact disc player. Shure Brothers is one of the leading manufacturers of phonograph cartridges and has experienced declining sales within the cartridge category. The compact disc player is an effort to steer the company in a new direction. The unit itself is a modified Sony deck. Courtesy of Shure Brothers.

tween the turntable, the cassette deck, and the new compact disc player, the salesperson let you hear first the crackling noise of the record, then the steady hiss of the cassette, and finally nothing at all from the CD player. He turned the volume halfway up and still not a sound—nothing—though the seconds were ticking on the timer on the player's faceplate. Then, with no warning, an explosive bass-drum erupted from the loudspeaker followed by a symphony orchestra playing at gale force. You listened for a while till a break came in the music and then the silence again.

The demonstration never failed to impress, and approximately 50,000 Americans bought the contraptions at an average of about $750 a crack the first year. Now, three years later, the price has come down to as low as $125, and the machines, now generally known as CD (compact disc) players, are selling by the hundreds of thousands. A scant 18 months after introduction, the compact disc player was accounting for more dollar volume at retail than was the traditional record player or turntable. Compact discs themselves were selling by the millions and, although records still outsold CDs at a ratio of 20:1, recording industry pundits were saying

CD sales would overtake those of phonograph records by late 1986 or 1987. Within both the audio hardware and the recording industries, numerous spokesmen were predicting that the phonograph would become obsolete sometime in the 1990s and that the compact disc would become the standard medium for recorded music in the home (Fig. 1-2).

In 1985, the year the compact disc really took off, such predictions began to be widely reported in the press, and millions of young Americans who had purchased stereo systems right out of school and hadn't visited a stereo store since, began to consider upgrading their systems. "You've got to switch over," the experts were saying. Phonograph records were going the way of the eight-track tape. Soon it would be CD or nothing.

As a trade journalist with several years of reporting for consumer electronic retailing publications, I believe that predictions of CD dominance sometime in the early 1990s are correct. I am not so certain that phonographs and phonograph records will disappear altogether within a decade, but they will lose ground rapidly to the new format. The manufacturing of phonographs is a declining industry, and major consumer electronics manufacturers, for the most part, are devoting no efforts to improving either the turntable or the phonograph record itself. Such technological stagnation is always a sign that a product is nearing the end of its lifespan. In the foreseeable future, digital recording will become the standard sound engineering technique in the record industry as well as in video and in motion pictures, and digital playback will become

Fig. 1-2. Matched Atelier system with CD player from ADS. CD players are easily integrated into most component stereo systems. Courtesy of ADS.

standard in home audio and possibly in home video, too.

The total impact of this digital revolution in sound is not entirely predictable. The chief advantages offered by digital recording and playback are relatively imperishable storage media and the possibility of duplicating recordings *ad infinitum*. What this means is that a digital recording, especially one that is stored on a compact disc, will not deteriorate with age. There is every reason to believe that a CD made today, scrupulously protected from dirt and scratches, and played hundreds of times will sound exactly the same 50 years from now. Phonograph records, on the other hand, obviously deteriorate with age and use—just try playing some old 78s from the 1940s—and so do analog magnetic tapes, though usually to a lesser extent. Digital recording permits musical performances to be preserved indefinitely with no increase in noise and no loss of high frequencies. Digital media and specifically the compact disc are archival.

The new technology of digital recording and transmission offers so many potential improvements and innovations in standard recording and broadcast practice that it's nearly impossible to predict the total impact that the digital revolution will have on the electronic mass media for the rest of the century. Every industry representing these media stands to be affected—the motion picture industry, certainly the recording industry, broadcast, cable and satellite television, radio, and prerecorded video. The rest of this chapter documents the courses of that revolution.

THE NATURE OF THE MEDIUM

The compact disc is a nonphotographic laser-scanned optical information storage medium digitally encoded with data on audio frequency waveforms. Such a definition might not mean much to anyone but an electronics engineer, but it does summarize most of what's peculiar to the format. Now, let me redefine this in plain English.

Notice we began by pronouncing the compact disc to be an *information storage medium*. That's not just empty verbiage. The consumer compact disc can be used to record pictures as well as sounds, and the basic disc itself can be inscribed with virtually any digital code and, thus, can carry any information that can be expressed in digital form. To put it another way, the basic disc can be used to record any sort of data that can be placed on the magnetic hard and floppy discs used in most computers. Both the digital encoding scheme and the actual recording track used in the standard consumer compact disc are specifically tailored to audio recording, but the blank disc itself imposes no physical restrictions preventing the use of other digital codes for other purposes. In fact, the computer industry is hard at work developing optical discs for industrial applications (Fig. 1-6).

I have stated that the compact disc is a nonphotographic laser-scanned optical recording medium. Again, this places the compact disc within a larger context. Since Edison invented the phonograph in 1878, four basic means have been devised for recording sound. Those means are:

• Mechanical storage which is the form of the phonograph where a pattern of ripples in the record groove carries the information on the recorded sounds.

• Magnetic recording where a magnetic field of varying strength is induced in a magnetic substance; generally a plastic tape coated with powdered metal or metal oxide, and exemplified by the audio cassette and the reel-to-reel audio tapes.

• Capacitive recording where a series of electrical charges on an electrically conductive surface are used to encode an audio signal, a means exemplified by the obsolete capacitance electronic disk collimator video disc (CED).

• Optical recording, which is probably the most mysterious to most people.

Optical recording employs a process whereby sound waves are made to produce variations in the intensity of a beam of light that is shone upon the recording medium. The recording blank used to make individual recordings is made to move beneath the beam of light so that different areas of its surface are progressively exposed to varying light values.

The simplest type of optical recording is a process of winding a strip of motion picture film stock past a light beam that flickers in time with the pulses of the sound waves being recorded. The sound waves are converted into electrical pulses that modulate the current supplying the light filament. Alternately, light falling on the film can be interrupted by a sound activated ribbon vibrating in a light aperture. The variations in exposure on the photographic film—the alternation of light and dark—will be preserved on the photographic positive that itself can later be used to interrupt another light beam. The second light beam is directed at an *electric eye* which, in turn, produces variations in electrical energy according to the intensity of light falling upon it. These varying electrical voltages can then be fed into an audio amplifier which, in turn, can reproduce the original sound through a loudspeaker. Optical recording of this type can be described as making a movie of sound and has been widely used in the motion picture industry for producing movie sound tracts.

The compact disc works on the same fundamental principle as a simple optical movie sound recording—that is, the spinning disc causes interruptions in a beam of light directed onto it. The optical mechanism employed in a compact disc player is a good deal more complex than the one on a movie projector and, more important, the compact disc itself is not film stock and contains no photographic representations on its surface. Physically, a compact disc is essentially similar to a phonograph record. It carries its information in the form of a series of tiny indentations arranged in a thin spiral that scrolls over the plane of the disc. The indentations cause variations of light and shadow as the beam of light sweeps over them, and an electric eye in the path of the reflected light beam registers the changes in light intensity as electrical pulses.

Now, in the case of the simple movie sound systems, the electrical pulses from the "eye" can, after amplification, be fed directly into a loudspeaker from which recorded sounds will then emerge. The photographic movie sound type of optical recording actually captures sound waves more or less directly onto film. The compact disc carries no direct representations of sound waves but, instead, contains a lot of digitally encoded information about the sound waves, or, to put it another way, a set of instructions that tells a decoder how to assemble replicas of the original sound waves. A compact disc player bears more than a passing resemblance to an electronic synthesizer. In a sense, it reproduces recorded sounds but in a very roundabout way, whereby sound waves are analyzed and characterized and put back together again. There are several very good reasons for all this complexity.

The light beam itself, which is used to scan a compact disc, is a laser beam rather than simply the ray of white light used in movie sound projectors. The tracks of indentations on a compact disc are microscopic and only an extremely narrow, highly focused light source will serve.

The disc itself is rotated on a platter like a phonograph record but is spun a good deal more rapidly. Elaborate servo mechanisms are used to focus the laser beam on the spiral and keep it in focus. Unlike a phonograph record, a compact disc has no groove wall to guide the transducer, which is the mechanism that picks up information from the recording medium and converts it into electrical impulses. The compact disc was deliberately designed so that there would be no physical contact between the transducer and the disc, so that the act of playing the disc would produce no wear. The indentations read by the laser beams could have been placed at the bottom of a groove and the groove walls themselves used to keep the laser beam in focus but, eventually, friction on the groove walls would have worn them down and resulted in the destruction of the disc. The developers of the compact disc wanted a permanent rather than a disposable recording medium, so they exerted considerable efforts to develop an automatic tracking system based on sensors rather than mechanical guidance.

HOW IT CAME TO BE

The compact disc was the product of many hands. It was not a case of some lone entrepreneur coming up with a brilliant invention and then attempting to sell it to the public. Marketing considerations rather than creative passion led to the development of the compact disc. High-level international conferences among the giants of the consumer electronics industry preceded the final development work, and the market niche that the new format would occupy was determined long before a working prototype existed.

The compact disc was the product of an intensive research and development program that, itself, was undertaken for a number of reasons. Foremost among them was the desire of the major manufacturers to promote overall growth in consumer audio from which (almost) all would benefit.

To provide a little historical background on the development of the compact disc, let's go back for a moment to the late 1940s when the high fidelity industry really emerged. Without a high fidelity industry, the compact disc would have remained in the laboratory—if it had ever been developed in the first place.

The high fidelity industry is one devoted to the sale of component audio systems—separate sound source, separate amplifier, and freestanding full-range loudspeakers. The basic equipment used in modern component audio systems was developed in the late 1920s, but component audio as a consumer product only came to the fore in the years immediately following World War II. In those days, England and America were the leaders in the world hi-fi industry, with Japan, the current leader, as yet having little influence beyond its own shores.

By the middle 1950s, high fidelity had become a major growth

7

industry in the United States, and millions of Americans owned electronic phonographs, whether of the console variety or of the more sophisticated component system type. Still in all, hi-fi systems remained rather expensive through the 1950s and early 1960s, particularly those of the superior component type. Ownership of audio equipment beyond a simple table radio remained fairly restricted even in affluent America.

The development of the relatively durable long play record in 1948 and the stereo long play record 10 years later were the major product developments during the first great age of high fidelity. Both contributed to major growth spurts, but by the early 1960s the industry was becoming mature in Europe and America and growth was leveling off. The cost of audio equipment remained high because its manufacture involved a lot of skilled and semiskilled labor by highly paid workers and a lot of expensive parts, particularly vacuum tubes. In marketing terms, the limits of its penetration appeared to have been reached.

Beginning about 1959, a trickle of Japanese audio goods began to arrive in the United States, at first mostly pocket-sized transistor radios. Then, in the early and middle 1960s, the Japanese began to apply the transistor approach to component audio and to sell component systems at prices that were substantially below English and American vacuum tube equipment. Japanese manufacturers such as Sony, Sansui, and Pioneer soon achieved enormous sales with this inexpensive solid-state gear, and by the late 1960s, Japan dominated the audio industry in Europe, Asia, and America.

The early solid-state audio boom lasted about 10 years. By the early 1970s, the industry was experiencing a decelerating growth pattern once again. The Japanese audio industry had grown initially with the impetus provided by low-cost, solid-state electronics. As the impetus was lost, several companies—principally Denon, Sansui, and JVC—attempted to reignite the audio boom with quadraphonic sound which, of course, failed catastrophically on the world market.

THE ADVENT OF DIGITAL RECORDING

Meanwhile, other Japanese companies were pursuing new courses, courses which would ultimately converge in the compact disc project.

During the late 1960s, a number of Japanese companies, including Sony, Nippon, Columbia (Denon), and NHK made the determination that a fundamental improvement in the phonograph record was in order, an improvement that would result in reproduction that was more lifelike.

Two such improvements suggested themselves at the time. The first, which was in some ways a step backwards, was called stereophonic direct-to-disk recording. Since the late 1940s, practically all phonograph records were actually transfers from tape recordings. Such transfers inevitably involved some loss of fidelity, but they greatly simplified the recording process by permitting the recording engineer to edit. In 1967, Denon in Japan and Doug Sax in the United States began independently to record live performances directly onto a master disk by feeding the signal from the microphone right into a record-cutting lathe. The stereo recordings resulting from this technique could be amazingly lifelike—sometimes almost indistinguishable from live feed taken directly from a microphone.

The direct-to-disk stereophonic recording was considered by many to be the ultimate audio storage medium, surpassing even the best first-generation, open-reel tape recordings, but the technique of direct-to-disk recording never became very popular because of the demands it placed on both performers and the recording engineer. One whole side of the disk had to be recorded in one take with no edits, and generally three to five cutting lathes were run simultaneously because each master could only produce about 25,000 records. The technique was expensive and totally impractical for million selling records. The major Japanese audio companies made a few disks for demonstration purposes, but never placed much faith in the process, and most of the direct-to-disk records actually released to the public were the products of small, independent record labels.

The second course for improving reproduction involved a then experimental technique known as digital recording. Digital recording is a subspecies within a larger family of recording techniques known as *modulation systems*. All of these techniques involve the superimposition of the audio signal proper onto another signal that is higher in frequency and is known as a *carrier*. The carrier will be held constant to some value—whether it be phase, amplitude, frequency or whatever—and the audio signal will modulate the carrier, producing various fluctuations in amplitude, phase, frequency, or whatever value is not being held constant. Modulation was originally developed back in the opening years of the century as a means of impressing an audio frequency signal on very high-frequency radio waves and, thus, transmitting sound electromagnetically through the atmosphere.

In the course of time, engineers found that modulation brought other benefits, one of which was expanded dynamic range. In other words, the capacity for recording sound waves of a greater range of intensity than could be recorded within a given medium in unmodulated form. Another benefit was a decrease in information losses in the course of transmitting the signal. Modulation could actually help to preserve the integrity of the signal.

Modulation techniques, themselves, may be divided into two basic classes: continuous wave parameter modulation systems and pulse parameter modulation systems. The former are analog in nature and the latter are digital. The differences between them are described in greater detail in Chapter 4, but for now I will simply define analog signals as infinitely variable fluctuations in continuously flowing waveforms, and digital signals as a kind of code consisting of a series of discrete pulses in which two conditions, on or off, pulse or no pulse, define the basic elements used to form the code. Morse code can be described as a sort of digital transmission, albeit on a more primitive level. Common analog modulation systems include AM and FM radio transmission (Fig. 1-3).

Several of the digital or pulse modulation techniques are theoretically superior to any of the analog varieties for storing and transmitting information. This might seem somewhat surprising because sound itself is more in the nature of an analog phenomenon; that is, it is an infinitely variable, continuously flowing series of waves.

Unfortunately, the recording of sound waves electrically in analog form cannot be done without introducing distortions in the signal. Such distortions increase with each electronic component the signal passes through within an analog circuit, and, to keep distortions at a minimum, each component within the signal chain must be as accurate as possible.

To give an obvious example, most telephone calls are transmitted in analog form, and a call to another continent passes through many circuits indeed. As we all know, such transcontinental calls are noisy at best, and sometimes almost unintelligible. In digital transmission, on the other hand, electronics circuits don't require highly accurate components because the circuits are made up of switches that need only turn on or off to produce the pulses employed in the code and needn't reproduce any fine graduations of intensity. The modulation system is what ensures accuracy, not the linearity of the signal circuits.

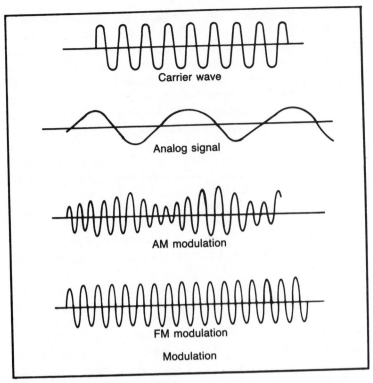

Carrier wave

Analog signal

AM modulation

FM modulation

Modulation

Fig. 1-3. Some modulation systems.

In order to produce recognizable sounds, digital circuits must eventually convert information into analog form and the special circuits used to perform this conversion must be very accurate indeed. As long as the information is kept within the digital code, however, it will theoretically remain completely intact during the process of recording and transmission. To put it another way, in the process of digital recording, sound is stored in the same general way that information is input into a computer memory and, in fact, a compact disc player is endowed with limited computing functions. In that respect, it is very different from the traditional phonograph.

Pulse modulation of sound was first employed in transmissions in the 1930s and digital recording of sound was first attempted at Massachusetts Institute of Technology in the mid 1950s. The technology of the time was wholly inadequate for the development of any practical digital audio format, but the theoretical possibilities of the process were understood. Research continued intermittently at various institutions until the late 1960s.

By the end of the 1960s, a breakthrough was possible due to changes in the physical forms of the recording media. For reasons that are explained in Chapter 4, digital recording of audio signals requires several times the information storage capacity of unmodulated analog recordings of equivalent bandwidth. In other words, the bandwidth of a digitalized audio signal is actually far greater than the audio waves themselves. Thus, the recording medium must be able to record frequencies many times higher than those of audible sound.

Until the 1960s a cost-effective recording medium capable of handling such high frequencies simply did not exist. Therefore, digital recording remained impractical.

A change came with the advent of practical video tape recorders in the early 1960s. Such devices were intended for recording very high frequency television signals, but they served equally well for recording digitized audio signals. Video tape technology made digital recording practical.

Long before the compact disc appeared, certain record companies and broadcasters began to record music digitally on magnetic tape (Fig. 1-4). By the early 1970s, Denon of Japan and the British Broadcasting Corporation were both making such recordings, and Denon was using them as master tapes for phonograph records. Denon did not advertise the digital origins of its phonograph records at that time.

In 1977, a handful of record labels, most notably Telarc, began to produce and promote such digitally mastered records, and the records themselves sold well in spite of premium pricing. Today, digital mastering is employed in almost all classical music releases and in an increasing number of popular recordings—although still a minority of the latter.

Much confusion still surrounds the subject of digitally mastered phonograph records. It might be well to explain just what these precursors to the compact disc really were.

As indicated earlier, LP records, except for rare direct-to-disk type, are all cut from tape recordings rather than from a live performance. These tape recordings, until the 1970s, were invariably of the ordinary, analog, reel-to-reel variety. Phonograph records made from such tapes are called simply analog phonograph records. The disc-cutting recording process used to make LPs is, itself, an analog technique. An analog record is analog through and through.

A digital phonograph record, on the other hand, is not digital through and through. A conventional analog disc-cutting process

Fig. 1-4. Early studio digital tape recorder. The control console in the background is an analog design. Courtesy of Sony Corporation.

is used to make the master lacquer for the record, and the digital tape recording that is played into the cutting lathe actually produces an analog signal at output. That output is free from some of the distortions present in an unmodulated analogue tape recording, but it is nonetheless analog and not digital. (All digital tape recorders in current use contain circuits known as digital-to-analog convertors that convert digitized signals into their analog counterparts.) It is possible to inscribe a digital signal directly onto a phonograph lacquer, but a specially configured cutting lathe and an extremely high rotation speed are required. Such all-digital phonograph records were developed experimentally in Germany in the late 1970s, as rivals to the yet unreleased compact disc format, but were never marketed. Needless to say, these fully digital phonograph records were completely incompatible with conventional records and could not be played on standard phonographs.

Digitally mastered phonograph records were initially presented to the public as a practical alternative to direct-to-disk recordings. Supposedly, the digital tape recording process involved virtually no losses or distortion of the audio information, and, thus, the recordings produced were said to be virtually identical to direct-to-disk recordings in terms of fidelity. Such, at any rate, were the claims of the record companies. Not all listeners or reviewers agreed, however.

13

Direct-to-disk recordings had been generally acknowledged to be sonically superior to ordinary records, although the performances themselves, which were usually recorded by small labels and involved lesser known artists, were frequently less impressive than the sonics. But digital phonograph records, while generally favorably received by critics and consumers alike, did not enjoy the universal praise that had greeted direct-to-disk. A small number of dissenters claimed that digital recordings sounded cold, harsh, artificial, and unpleasant. Dissent, in fact, continues to this day, and similar objections have been leveled against the compact disc. We will explore the digital controversy more fully in Chapter 6, but in relating the development of the compact disc it is sufficient to say that minority objections to digital sound have had almost no impact on marketability of either compact discs or digitally mastered phonograph records. Both have been phenomenally successful.

By the time digital records began to sell in large numbers, the major Japanese audio companies were already meeting in earnest to develop a standard for the present compact disc format. In 1978, Philips and Sony proposed something very close to the existing compact disc format to the Japan Electronics Industries Association, a very powerful Japanese trade group that currently plays a major role in determining the collective course of the worldwide consumer electronics industry. The JEIA established a standards committee which set the current standards in 1980. The first commercial compact disc players appeared in Japan two years later.

In a sense, the digital phonograph record can be seen then as a promotional overture for the compact disc. The compact disc represented such a departure from existing analog formats that the major Japanese manufacturers felt the public should first be educated as to the virtues of digital sound. Many of the same companies that later made compact disc players begin making digital tape recorders for studio use in the late 1970s. These companies loudly proclaimed the onset of the digital age as they began to sell digital tape recorders to the major record labels who, in turn, used them to produce *digital phonograph records*. But the step from the digitally mastered phonograph record to the compact disc involved a minor revolution in playback technology and would not have been possible but for a development in analog recording that preceded the introduction of digital recording in the record industry by several years. That development was the laser scanned optical disc.

THE DEVELOPMENT OF LASER SCANNING

The idea of using beams of laser light to pick up information recorded on a disc was first conceived in the 1960s very soon after the creation of the first industrial lasers (patents were filed as early as the 1930s for prelaser optical pickup systems for phonograph records). The first use of lasers as audio pickup devices was as substitutes for phonograph style. The laser beam was directed along the grooves of conventional phonograph records, and the shadows cast by the ripples in the groove walls interrupted the beam and caused varying voltages in a photo eye that received the reflected beam. The laser pickup, of course, was frictionless and the record itself incurred no wear from being played.

The idea was intriguing, but experiments along this line were not encouraging. Some experiments with laser optical phonograph pickups were performed in Japan in the late 1960s and early 1970s, but as yet no practical laser optical systems for phonograph records has been demonstrated. Nevertheless, a small California-based research firm called Finial has announced a working prototype and plants to market it sometime in late 1986.

Lack of progress in this area persuaded the Japanese manufacturers that an entirely new disc format would be required to make laser tracking feasible. In 1972 just such a format appeared.

This format, which was the direct ancestor of the compact disc, was the laser-optical video disc that still survives today in the Laserdisc format. Because the laser optical video disc is still sometimes confused with the compact disc, and because it paved the way for the latter, it merits a brief description.

Video discs, in one form or another, go back to the dawn of television in the late 1920s, but the laser scanned optical version first surfaced in 1972 when Philips and MCA, by a remarkable coincidence, announced prototypes that were independently developed and, at the same time, essentially identical.

The Philips-MCA machine, that closely resembled the present-day Pioneer Laserdisc player, used an iridescent 12-inch disc, which looked like a blown-up CD and rotated at an average rate of 1800 rpm (unlike a record but like a CD, a laser disc is scanned from the label outward, and the speed of rotation progressively slows so that the velocity of the track passing over the pickup remains the same at all times (Fig. 1-5)). In the current Laserdisc format the track, which is spiral in form, contains a succession of elliptically shaped pits of varying lengths that are cut into the flat sur-

Fig. 1-5. Pioneer Artists Laserdisc. The Laserdisc resembles the compact disc physically, but it's bigger—12 inches across for the standard size, and 8 inches for the new "video 45". Courtesy of Pioneer Artists.

face of the polycarbonate substrate. The substrate is coated with aluminum foil, to make it reflective, and then it is also coated with a tough, clear plastic to protect it.

The pits reflect little light while the flat sections are highly reflective. As the track passes under the laser beam, the reflected beam goes bright and dim—pulses, in effect. A photo diode converts the variations in light intensity into varying electrical voltages. A complex series of servomechanisms maintains steady groove velocity and keeps the beam in focus.

The basic electrical mechanical systems employed to spin the disc and focus the laser pickup are very similar to those employed in a compact disc player and, indeed, provide the model for the latter. The differences between the two mainly involve the type of information stored on the disc and the method of storage.

Obviously, a Laserdisc carries moving pictures as well as a sound track, but, more important, it carries the information in analog form. The pits carry an FM (frequency modulated) signal where only the frequency of the signal varies and amplitude remains constant. However, frequency is infinitely variable and the actual length of the pits themselves is within certain limits infinitely variable as well. This is not the case with compact disc where the pits assume a finite number of discrete dimensions.

The FM system used to encode pictures and sound on a Laserdisc is essentially similar to the types of systems used for broadcasting radio and television signals or for storing information on a video cassette. An FM demodulator is used to recover the audio and video signals. The system employs different carrier frequencies and bandwidths from those used in broadcast applications, but the principle is the same.

Industry-wide standards for the laser optical video disc were set in 1976 but, even before that time, the possibilities of employing the system for digital audio-only recording were being widely discussed. By 1975, industry insiders believed that the Japan Electronics Industries Association would eventually approve some kind of laser-scanned digital audio disc. At the time, however, the optical disc wasn't the only storage medium in the running for use in a consumer digital format.

In any case, Philips decided to produce its laser video disc system before releasing a laser-scanned audio disc. It released a laser-scanned video disc player in 1978 through Magnavox, its North American subsidiary. Pioneer, under a licensing agreement with MCA, released an industrial version of the machine in the same year. Neither machine created much of a stir at the time, but two years later Pioneer brought out its own consumer version, which the company called Laservision, amidst a concerted publicity campaign. Laservision was not and is not recordable, and in spite of superior sound and picture quality, the format did not do well commercially against the emergent home video-cassette formats. Nevertheless, Laservision, later called Laserdisc, survives to this day, and currently some of the discs have digital sound tracks and some of the players also have digital decoders. The digital versions of the Laserdisc are discussed in Chapter 9.

One of the minor curiosities of the whole Laserdisc interlude before the coming of the compact disc was the failure of the industry to introduce an audio-only version. An FM encoded audio-only Laserdisc could have been feasibly introduced in the early 1970s and the FM encoding process offered at least potentially better sound than that available on phonograph records, plus the added benefit of frictionless playback. Engineers had decades of experience in designing high fidelity FM circuits whereas digital audio circuits were still highly problematic at the time. Why didn't the industry go with proven FM technology? Why did the industry hold back for a full 10 years before finally releasing a laser-scanned audio disc in a digital configuration?

The leaders of the Japanese consumer electronics industry are notably closed-mouthed about the reasons for their decisions. A number of obvious explanations suggest themselves.

First of all, the industry was in chaos in the early 1970s due to the simultaneous introduction of several incompatable quadraphonic record formats, and the consumer was wary of any new format. The time wasn't right. Secondly, digital encoding offers theoretically higher fidelity than FM encoding. Like all analog audio systems, FM encoding cannot prevent progressive information losses at each stage in the circuit. For the utmost clarity in a disc format, any FM system requires either noise reduction circuits, which always function imperfectly, or extremely accurate rotation of the platter supporting the disc, which entails costly precision machinery in the player. Thirdly, error correction as opposed to noise reduction is virtually impossible in the analog domain and, indeed, dropouts have been a persistent problem with the Laserdisc. Matching digital performance with FM circuitry at a given price point seemed difficult or impossible.

The other persuasive argument favoring digital was the possibility of keeping information within the digital domain during the amplification process and avoiding analog information losses up to the point when the signal is ready to be sent to the loudspeaker. Digital amplifiers, described in some detail in Chapter 10, were first developed in the late 1960s. They appeared to represent the technology of the future 15 years ago when Japanese industry leaders first began to ponder the replacement to the phonograph.

At any rate, the Japanese were strongly inclined toward something like the compact disc by about 1976, and once industry standards had been agreed upon in 1980, the way was fairly clear for an introduction. The three-year delay was more the result of worldwide economic recession and the problems of tooling up for mass production than any fundamental problems with the new format. Nevertheless, a number of companies, most significantly Hitachi and JVC, attempted to introduce rival digital audio discs based on capacitative systems. Capacitative discs that store information in the form of *electrets*—permanent charges of electricity on the disc's surface—are much less expensive to manufacture than compact discs, and the playback mechanism for reproducing them is extremely simple and inexpensive. Unfortunately, capacitative discs do wear out with repeated playings and lack the high-tech image that is so important in marketing a new format. Neither rival format ever got off the ground.

Fig. 1-6. CD-ROM, courtesy of Digital Equipment Corporation.

The history of the compact disc following its introduction is more a story of marketing strategy than further technical developments. Certain circuit refinements have been introduced in certain players, but the basic design of the CD player seems unlikely to change much for the remainder of its product life (Fig. 1-7).

As for the marketing campaign on behalf of the new format, an entire book could be written about that. Sony and Philips, who

Fig. 1-7. Sony CDP 55 Compact Disc Player. This unit which includes non-resonant cerasin cabinet, low mass laser pickup, and digital filtering, cost under $400 retail and demonstrates the dramatic price reductions which have occurred in the 3 years since the players were introduced. Courtesy of Sony Corporation.

held most of the patents, licensed the CD technology to dozens of manufacturers. In addition, most of the major record labels formed a trade association, called the Compact Disc Group, to promote the new format. The promotion was successful beyond anything in the entire history of audio, going back to the invention of the phonograph. No new consumer format has made profit so quickly.

Unfortunately, this grand promotional effort did little to educate the public on the true potential and limitations of the new medium, how best the players could be incorporated in a home audio system, or what qualitative differences existed among players themselves. I don't think I flatter myself by suggesting that this book fulfills a real need.

Chapter 2

Basic
Construction and Operation

A compact disc player is a fairly intricate piece of machinery containing many times more circuit elements than a phonograph or cassette deck. It uses a very complicated mechanical system for rotating the platter that supports the disc, and for aiming the laser pickup that scans the information contained on the disc. You certainly don't have to understand the workings of a compact disc player to use and enjoy one, but a basic understanding of its construction is helpful when making a purchase, especially if you're considering one of the more expensive machines.

THE SOFTWARE

To understand how players are put together, you first have to have some comprehension of how information is stored on the disc and how the disc is structured.

Compact discs are compact indeed, measuring a mere 120 millimeters in diameter, or about 4.75 inches across—a little over a third the size of an ordinary 12-inch, long-playing phonograph record. The thickness is 1.2 millimeters, the center hole is 15 millimeters across, and the weight is roughly 14 grams. Unlike the phonograph record, a CD never comes in odd sizes. The form is completely standardized, including track width, eccentricity of track radius, etc. Maximum playing time is 74 minutes, but an hour or less of program material is more typical.

In physical construction, the compact disc is very different from a phonograph record. The compact disc is a single-sided medium and the blank face carries the label. In cross section, the compact disc is a sandwich with a substrate made of a polycarbonate substance, a very thin layer of aluminum over that, and finally a tough, clear acrylic coating over the aluminum.

The information on the disc is carried beneath the clear surface within a single spiral track made up of tiny oblong *pits* separated by level spaces called *flats* (Fig. 2-1). The pits are stamped into the polycarbonate substrate much as phonograph record grooves are stamped, and the reflective aluminum coating follows the contours of the pits and flats. All pits are exactly the same depth, 0.11 micrometers, but they vary in length. Unlike the pits in the related Laservision format, they can only assume a finite number of discrete lengths, length is not infinitely variable.

The pits appear as dark shadows to the laser eye that scans them. The flats, in contrast, are highly reflective. The contrasting light values produced by the reflection of the laser beam on the pits and the flats represent the basic on-off conditions necessary to construct a digital code. However, the pits and flats are not equivalent to single "bits" of information—to use computer terminology. Simple one-to-one correspondence between bits and pits would require a disc several times the size of the current format, one that could hardly be termed compact. Instead, subcodes are

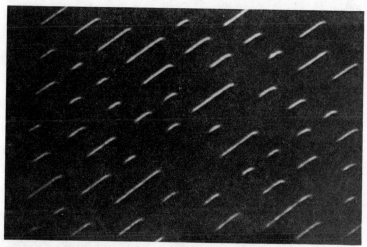

Fig. 2-1. A representation of the audio track on a compact disc clearly showing pits and flats. Courtesy of Sony Corporation.

employed in compact disc recording that designate specific multibit values to pits of various lengths.

The compact disc has no groove per se. Each loop of the spiral is separated by a distance which varies from 0.833 to 3.054 micrometers—the same dimension as the pits themselves. The space between spirals is level, not elevated, and there are no groove walls to guide the pickup. The track is read from the center of the disc outward, just the opposite of a conventional phonograph record.

The compact disc, like the Laserdisc, has a variable speed of rotation. Speed varies from 500 rpm at the inner groove to 200 rpm at the outer edge of the disc. Obviously, a single revolution of the disc brings a greater length of track beneath the pickup at the outer edge than near the center, so variable rotation speed is needed to provide constant velocity.

Compact discs are supposed to be completely flat, but, like phonograph records, they are subject to warpage, especially in conditions of extreme heat. Severe warping can adversely affect tracking and can even damage the pickup, and for this reason, a few machines include clamps to hold the disc tight against the platter.

COMPACT DISC PLAYERS—BASIC CONSTRUCTION

The compact disc player has been described as a highly specialized form of the turntable. Both play discs of prerecorded audio program material—discs that are not themselves rerecordable. Both also employ rotating platters to support the disc, and both use a moving pickup to scan a spiral track in sequential fashion. But a phonograph, at its most basic, contains no electronic circuits. It's a relatively simple device consisting of platter to hold the record, a motor that rotates the platter, and a base to which the platter and motor are attached. An integrated turntable adds a *tonearm* and a *cartridge*, the former being a light rod or beam sweeping over the surface of the record, and the latter being a tiny electrical generator that produces electrical current from the motions of the needle or stylus tracing the record groove. The best turntables reflect some very sophisticated engineering in the areas of vibration damping and bearing design, but except for the linear tracking variety, turntables are fundamentally very simple mechanisms (Fig. 2-2).

The compact disc player has a base, motor, and a platter but it has much more as well. Let's start with the mechanical system.

Home compact disc players follow two basic mechanical designs: top loading and front loading. The front loading group is sub-

Fig. 2-2. Micro Seiki RX-1500FVG, one of the world's finest turntables. This unit includes a vacuum pump to hold records firmly to the platter, and an air bearing for lowest possible friction. Massive bronze and zinc castings are used throughout to reduce resonance, and system weight is over 100 pounds. Yet compared to a compact disc player, this component is mechanically very simple. Courtesy of Analog Excellence.

divided into drawer, tray, and vertical front load types. The mechanical parts are somewhat different in each type.

Top load players, which are presently sold only by Sony, Technics, Meridian, and Bang & Olufsen, load very much like a conventional turntable. You raise a lid on the top of the player, that corresponds to the turntable's dustcover, and insert a disc onto the platter manually. You then close the lid and commence play (Fig. 2-3).

In the drawer-type frontloader, the platter and optical pickup are contained within a sliding drawer. To load the player you pull the drawer out, place the disc on the platter, and slide the drawer back into the machine (Fig. 2-4). The tray type is similar except that the sliding element is simply a carrier and contains neither the platter nor pickup. A loading motor automatically positions the disc for play when the tray is returned to the machine. Over 95 percent of the machines on the market today employ either the drawer or tray loading methods.

With the vertical front loading scheme, the disc surface faces the listener and rotates vertically like a wagonwheel. A clamp holds the disc to the platter. Hitachi favored this loading scheme initially, but today only Kyocera markets a vertical, front-loading player.

OPTICS

Beyond the variety of loading arrangements, players differ

24

Fig. 2-3. Bang & Olufsen CDX Compact Disc Player, one of the few top loaders in existence. Courtesy of Bang & Olufsen.

mechanically in the design of the laser pickup. Virtually all home CD players use the same general arrangement of lenses and prisms to aim and project the laser beam, but the manner in which the laser pickup is positioned over the surface of the disc will differ from player to player following two basic models: the rotating arm design and the sliding pickup.

The rotating arm type of pickup is somewhat similar in form

to the tonearm on a conventional phonograph. The pickup is mounted at the free end of a beam that is supported at the other end by a pivoting base. The free end swings laterally in a shallow arc across the disc much like an ordinary tonearm, though rather than being guided by grooves, it is steered by a complex automatic tracking system. The rotating arm is generally employed in top-load and front-load players.

The slide or sled type of pickup places the laser assembly on a sliding carrier that moves the laser beam across the surface of the disc in a straight line. There is no pivoting base. The mechanism somewhat resembles a certain type of linear tracking tonearm used in conventional turntables. The slide type of pickup generally appears in tray-loading and vertical front-loading players.

Whatever the pickup design, the pickup itself always reads information from below, and the disc is actually played upside down. The pickup itself is a relatively bulky mechanism complete with its own motors and control circuitry, and it's much easier to place the pickup within the body of the machine rather than poised over the disc. The pickup is the key mechanical part of a compact disc player and it is worth examining in some detail.

Both rotary and slide type pickups use essentially similar mechanisms for focusing the laser beam on the disc and picking up its reflections; only the carrier for the laser emitter and receptor are different.

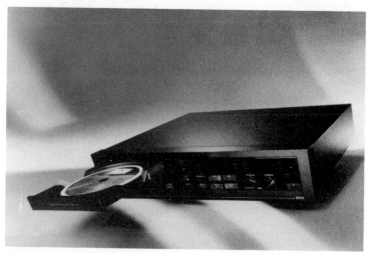

Fig. 2-4. Dbx DX3 drawer loading compact disc player with drawer extended. Courtesy of Dbx.

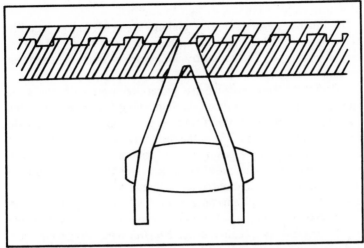

Fig. 2-5. Laser beam directed up toward the audio track of a compact disc. Courtesy of Sony.

All consumer compact disc players use what is known as a solid-state laser consisting of a special form of light-emitting diode. The laser itself is a beam of coherent light, which means that all of the light rays in the beam are of precisely the same frequency and in phase with one another. A laser beam is much more desirable for use in optical pickup systems than ordinary white light because the laser beam is particularly intense and highly focused and can register changes in reflectivity over extremely small surface areas.

The laser diode used in a compact disc player is mounted on the sled or rotary arm and is aimed straight up at the underside of the compact disc itself, and it alternately strikes reflective flats and dark pits as the disc moves past it (Fig. 2-5). When the beam strikes a flat, most of the light is reflected off of the aluminum surface and ultimately registered by a receptor. In digital terms, this constitutes the on condition. But when the light strikes a pit, an out-of-phase reflection from the bottom of the pit causes a momentary cancellation of the light waves so that very little reflected light reaches the laser eye. This represents the off condition.

Before the laser beam reaches the underside of the disc, it first must pass through a complex system of lenses and a prism; these focus and guide the laser beam to and from the surface of the disc and then ultimately to the photodiode, which receives the reflected beam and reacts to the variations in light intensity by generating varying electrical voltages. The precise number and arrangement of lenses varies from one design to another.

Three basic types of optical pickups are in use in compact disc players: the radial tracking type, the rotary arm type, and the rotary mirror type. The radial tracking variety is by far the most common.

Radial tracking systems are generally used with sled-type pickups. The most significant distinguishing feature of the radial tracking system is the use of three separate laser beams—one to retrieve the audio signal from the disc, and two side beams to aid in tracking. The three-beam configuration is often mentioned in advertising copy and unquestionably provides for better tracking— that is, better alignment of the laser pickup with the audio track— than a single beam system can provide. The drawback to the three-beam system is that the two tracking beams are produced by sending the original laser beam through a *diffraction grating* which critically reduces the power of the central beam, the one that actually reproduces the audio track. This results in more light scatter within the reflective layer of the disc and a lessened ability to register imperfectly formed pits. Three beam systems track better but they make more errors when scanning the track. Thus, either system involves tradeoffs.

The diffraction grating is generally the first object encountered by the laser beam in a radial tracking system. From there it will go to the *half prism*, also known as a polarization beam splitter, which may be thought of as a kind of one way mirror angled at 45 degrees relative to the plane of the laser diode itself. The half prism permits the light emitted by the laser diode to pass straight through to the surface of the disc or, alternately, to another prism that then reflects the beams upward to the surface of the disc. The beams will be perfectly perpendicular to the disc surface and will be reflected straight back the way they came—that is, back into the half prism. (Remember that the prism is a one way mirror angled at 45 degrees.) When the reflected laser beams strike the half prism on the rebound, they are reflected at a 90 degree angle and directed to the photo diode. The photo diode registers the light intensity of the beams from moment to moment and generates appropriate matching voltages (Fig. 2-6).

But before the half prism can operate, the polarity of the reflected beams must be reversed from that of the direct beams. This operation is performed in the *one quarter wave length grating plate* which effects a reversal of polarity in the laser beams as they pass through it.

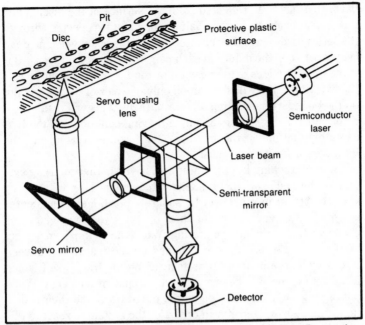

Fig. 2-6. Radial tracking optical pickup system. Courtesy of Sony Corporation.

In addition, a *collimator lens* will be placed at some point in the route of the beams to train the three beams along parallel paths. Just before the beams strike the disc, they must pass through the *objective lens* which focuses the beams directly on the spiral track and which is servo-controlled much like the autofocus on a camera. We shall have more to say on it in a moment.

After deflection by the half prism, the reflected beams will traverse a different series of lenses. These lenses will vary in number from one machine to another and are variously termed collective, cylindrical, concave, and convex lenses. They serve to focus the beams on the receptor diodes and assist in the process of detecting whether the track itself is in focus (Fig. 2-7).

All compact disc players, radial tracking and otherwise, are provided with an auto focusing system that keeps the outgoing laser beam from the laser diode light tightly focused on the track itself. The objective lens, essentially the back end of that system, is joined through a feedback loop to the photodiode receptors which provide the information for accurately focusing the objective lens.

Here's how the system works. The player is equipped with not one but four photodiodes grouped together to receive the central beam that has been reflected from the surface of the disc. When the central beam strikes the half prism and it is reflected through the series of lenses to the receptor diodes, the beam will land dead center between the diodes in each pair, if the laser is in focus. But if the objective lens is too near to, or too far from, the surface of the disc, the beam will shine upon only one pair of diodes and not on the boundary separating all four of them. This will result in an error signal being sent to a simple moving coil motor in the lens assembly that moves the lens back and forth. By this means, the lens is kept in perfect focus.

Radial tracking laser pickups also have another focusing system for the sled itself, that is intended to keep the laser in tangency with the track; in other words, squarely positioned dead center above it. Tangency is maintained by the two tracking beams produced by the diffractive grating. When the pickup is in perfect tangency, the side beams are trained on the flat areas between tracks while the main beam is focused on the track itself; when in tangency, the side beams produce a constant on-signal. When out of tangency, they intrude on the pitted track and their reflections diminish in intensity. In order for the system to react to this condition, each side beam has its own separate diode receptor that produces a correction signal when light intensity drops. A servo mechanism moves the optical assembly to the side and brings it back in tangency. All this must happen extremely rapidly or audible dropouts will be heard in the music.

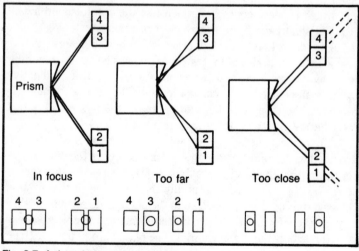

Fig. 2-7. A three-beam system in operation.

The rotary arm type pickup uses the same basic components as the slide type, but it generally only employs one beam, not two. The mechanism is somewhat simpler with fewer mirrors and lenses and a shorter, more direct path from laser diode to disc. In this system, the central beam is split twice during emission. The first split occurs at the level of the laser diode itself. A low-power secondary beam is emitted from the rear of the laser diode directly onto a receptor photodiode. This reception diode measures the intensity of the secondary beam and, by extension, that of the main beam; the purpose of this arrangement is to maintain a constant power level for the laser. Laser diodes are temperature sensitive and output tends to fluctuate. If a fluctuation is detected by the photodiode, a servo sends more current to the laser diode.

The laser beam is split a second time just before it strikes the main diode receptors for the audio signal; this process occurs in the half prism. In this system, two pairs of diodes are used just as in the three-beam system, but the pairs are separated and each beam is aimed at the boundary between the two diodes in each pair. Auto focusing is essentially the same as in the three-beam system—any departure of either beam from either boundary generates a correction signal. However, in this system, the two beams also serve the function of the tracking beams in the three-beam system. By most accounts, the tracking accuracy suffers as a result. Generally, in this system, the entire arm moves in response to error signals, unlike the slide optic system in which only the optical system itself moves (Fig. 2-8).

In the little used rotary mirror system, a movable mirror is placed between the lens system and the laser, and this is used to

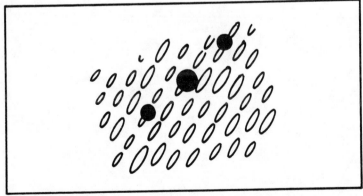

Fig. 2-8. Tracking system for a one beam optical pickup.

keep the beam in tangency. The system is faster than the others, but has not found much acceptance.

Compact disc players exhibit a high degree of mechanical complexity. Hundreds of high-tolerance moving parts are required for the assembly of the machines, and the fact that they can be sold at retail for as little as $100 is a tribute to Japanese industrial techniques. But if the mechanism is complicated, the circuitry required to decode the disc is even more so. Not until the advent of large-scale integrated circuits in the late 1970s did the machines become a feasible product on a consumer level.

Chapter 3

Sound and Audio Specifications

When the compact disc format was introduced, Phillips Corporation, its prime developer, made much use of the phrase "perfect sound forever" in promoting the new medium. Not provided in the Phillips advertisements was any definition of perfect sound or information as to what made the medium perfect. Critics of digital sound scoffed at the claims, and the public shrugged and bought compact disc players, all presumably perfect.

In this chapter, I attempt to examine the claims in some depth. In order to do that, I must first explain the nature of sound and of audio specifications.

SOUND

Sound, as is pretty generally understood, is a wave phenomenon. The behavior of sound waves follows similar principles to the visible waves that occur on the surface of a body of water, although the form of a sound wave is rather different from a surface wave on water. A sound wave traveling through the atmosphere is, by strictest definition, a variation in pressure within adjacent volumes of air. Usually, when sound waves are propagated, a vibrating solid body compresses the air next to its surface by virtue of its vibratory movements. Because air is elastic, the compressed volume of air springs back to its original volume and compresses an adjacent air mass more distant from the sound source. That air mass, in turn, springs back and compresses another air mass, and so on. The sound wave itself consists of a succession of a compressed and released air mass, and may be described as a pulse traveling outward from the sound source (Fig. 3-1).

One unfamiliar with the manner in which sound waves are propagated might object with the assertion that pressure cannot build up in an unenclosed volume of air because the air molecules immediately spread out evenly as they are disturbed. But, in fact, the vibratory movements that produce audible sound are on the order of 15 times per second minimally and as rapid as 20,000 times per second. At these speeds, the pressure builds up in the area adjacent to the vibratory surface faster than the air molecules can disperse and stabilize the air pressure within this adjacent volume of air. A mass of compressed air forms whose dimensions vary quite precisely according to the speed with which the sound producing body is vibrating, and that mass transfers its energy to another air mass that does likewise. Sound waves are nothing more than successions of pressurized masses of air interspersed with low pressure air masses of equal volume.

So how are these sound waves characterized and how is it determined whether the sound waves produced by an audio system are a good match for those produced in a live performance? They

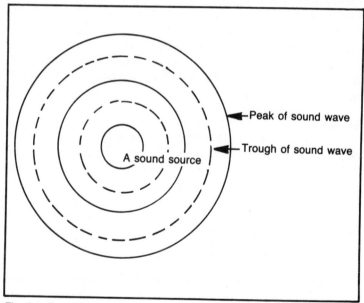

Fig. 3-1. Sound is propagated in concentric globes outward from the sound source.

are measured. All individual sound waves can be fully character-ized by only two measurements: *frequency*, and *intensity* or pressure.

Frequency

The frequency of a sound wave is just that—how frequently it will transfer its energy to an adjacent mass of air in a given period of time—conventionally one second. The frequency of the sound wave in air will exactly correspond to the frequency of the vibrat-ing body producing it. If, for instance, a tuning fork is made to vi-brate 262.83 times per second (Middle C), the air around it will pulse at the same frequency, and 261.83 wave peaks will have formed in a single second.

One should note that all sound waves of whatever frequency travel at the same speed, 1127 feet per second at sea level. (By travel we mean transfer their energy to adjacent air masses. The molecules next to the vibrating body do not themselves travel 1127 feet in one second.) Furthermore, all sound waves of a given fre-quency are exactly the same length, with lower frequency sound waves being longer than higher frequency waves (Fig. 3-2). (Keep in mind that the unit of time for measuring frequency is conven-tionally 1 second, and that the distance traveled by sound in that time span is 1127 feet.) Thus, a sound wave with a frequency of 15 Hertz (Hz), which signifies 15 cycles or pulses per second, will produce 15 pulses in one second and the fifteenth pulse will ex-tend to exactly 1127 feet away from the sound source. Since each pulse or wave is of equal length, the length of any one of them can be determined by dividing 1127 by 15 which gives us 75.13 feet. Therefore, a 15 Hz sound wave is 75.13 feet long. Correspondingly, a 20 Kilohertz sound wave, which is too high pitched for many per-sons to hear clearly, will produce 20,000 pulses in one second, the 20 thousandth of which also extends exactly 1127 feet from the sound source. By the same reckoning, each of those 20,000 waves is 0.056 feet or 0.6 inches in length (1127 ÷ 20,000).*

Soundwaves of a single unvarying frequency are known as *sine* waves, sine being short for sinusoidal. Such waves may be described as a smooth, regular alteration in air pressure. The peak of the wave is the period of highest pressure, and the trough is the period of lowest pressure. Between the peaks and troughs is a period of ex-

---

(*Footnote: The speed of sound varies slightly with altitude and air temperature. Speed increases with air temperature and decreases with altitude.)

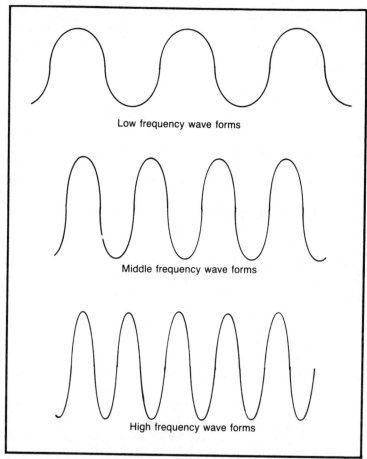

Low frequency wave forms

Middle frequency wave forms

High frequency wave forms

Fig. 3-2. Examples of sound waves.

act equilibrium called the *zero crossing* where air pressure is mid-way between peak and minimal values. Sine waves are conventionally represented by a scalloped pattern of peaks and valleys, with the zero crossing line dividing the curve so that equal portions of space are defined above and below the zero crossing line. Mathematically, the curves can be described by sinusoidal functions, hence the term sine wave (Fig. 3-3).

Pure sine waves can be generated electronically but almost never occur in natural sounds—though the sound of the modern flute comes fairly close to being purely sinusoidal. Instead, virtually all natural sounds are made up of combinations of sine waves occurring simultaneously. In musical sounds, the combinations are made

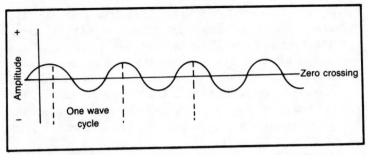

Fig. 3-3. Sine wave.

up of *harmonics*, an ascending order of sine waves with each tone spaced an octave apart, more or less (Fig. 3-4). Variations in the relative intensities of those harmonics determine the characteristic tonal qualities or timbres of each musical instrument.

Non musical sounds, termed noise, consist of combinations of sine waves in widely varying pitch relationships. According to the standard theory of sound which utilizes mathematical analysis first performed by Joseph Fourier in the early 19th century, all sounds, however complex, can be broken down into a series of sine waves.

Intensity

The second measurement, aside from frequency, that used to characterize sound waves, is pressure or intensity, which correlates

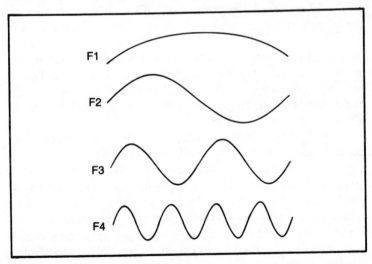

Fig. 3-4. Harmonic sine waves.

with perceived loudness and refers specifically to the air pressure within the high pressure masses that make up sound waves. However, the standard measure of sound pressure level does not employ pounds per cubic inches as does the measurement of gases in confined volumes. Rather, a unit called a *decibel* is employed.

A decibel is a confusing term for many people because it refers not to a fixed quantity but to a relationship between quantities, the ratio between two power levels to be precise. The decibel is formally defined as 10 log (P2/P1).

The terms 3 decibels, 13 decibels, or any number of decibels, are meaningless in and of themselves as measures of absolute intensity. A sound can be said to be 3 or 13 decibels more intense than another sound, but unless the value of one is defined in terms of mechanical force, the intensity of either sound is indeterminate. If this seems a little unclear, read on.

In consumer audio specifications, decibels most commonly define a relationship to a fixed reference level of sound, namely the softest sound that is audible to a person with good hearing. In terms of pressure level, this *zero decibel* reference level of force is stated to be 0.0002 microbar, with one microbar being equivalent to one millionth of normal atmospheric pressure. Therefore, a sound of 1 decibel (dB) is 1 decibel louder than the weakest audible sound.

Since decibels are logarithmic in function, an 8 dB increase in sound pressure level for example is not twice as loud as a 4 dB sound pressure level. Instead, whatever the sound pressure level, whether it be 1 dB or 100 dB, an addition of 3 dB signifies a doubling of the intensity or sound pressure. Thus, a sound of 103 dB is twice as intense as one of 100 dB. One should realize, moreover, that human hearing does not register increases in intensity proportionally, and that human hearing itself follows logarithmic patterns. To our ears, a 3 dB increase—that is a doubling of intensity—seems only slightly louder. A 10 dB increase is necessary to create an impression of approximate-doubling of loudness.

Generally when we refer to decibels in the text, we are assuming that sound pressure level is referenced to the 0.0002 microbar zero level, and in this sense, the decibel becomes an absolute measurement. Individuals who are knowledgable about audio habitually use decibels in this manner, and they tend to have very precise perceptions about what an 80 dB or 90 dB sound pressure levels is. If you spend much time auditioning equipment, you will soon develop a similar sense as to how various degrees of loudness translate into decibels.

```
           Decibels referenced to threshold of human
                    hearing and A-weighted

                        170
                        160
                        150
                        140  Threshold of pain
                        130
                        120  Discotheque
Cymbal maximum intensity 110  Jackhammer closeup
   Piano-maximum intensity 100  Electric furnace area
Trumpet-maximum intensity  90
                         80  Typical automobile interior at 60 mph
                         70   Average (rms) level of conversation
                         60
                         50
                         40  Quiet room
                         30
```

Fig. 3-5. Decibel levels.

A chart is included (Fig. 3-5) to indicate how various decibel levels relate to common sounds in the environment. Generally it can be said that most domestic audio systems operate at levels from about 70 dB to 105 dB. Anything over 90 dB will be perceived as pretty loud by most people, and anything over 105 dB will sound extremely loud.

Incidentally, sustained exposure to average sound pressure levels of over 100 dB can permanently damage hearing, so if you decide to purchase a high powered stereo system, do exercise caution.

Phase

Frequency and intensity fully define any individual sound wave, however, sound waves generally occur in multiples, many multiples, of wave following wave by the thousands. These succession of waves are related to one another in terms of *phase*, a frequently misunderstood word that comes up again and again in discussions of acoustics and audio electronics.

Phase refers to the relationship of two series of high and low pressure air masses to one another. To understand the nature of this relationship, one must go back to the concept of sine waves discussed earlier in this chapter. A single cycle of a sine wave beginning at the zero crossing, the point of equilibrium, describes an S curve as it first ascends to its peak value, falls down past the zero crossing to its lowest value, and then ascends once again to zero crossing where the cycle begins anew. This S curve contains 360 degrees, the same number of degrees as a circle and, thus, each wave peak is separated from its immediate neighbors by 360 degrees—provided, that is, that the wave is being propagated in unobstructed space. But what happens if, for example, the wave strikes an obstruction and the sound is reflected back? What happens is that a single succession or series of waves becomes, in effect, two series of waves, although the reflected and direct sounds are not entirely separate from one another but, rather, are intermingled with one another like eddies in a pond. During the intermingling, the phase relationship that is, the alignment of the two successions of waves, determines the sound pressure level represented by their sum. If two series of waves line up exactly, they are said to be in phase or in a zero phase relationship. In such instances, the sound intensity becomes the sum of the separate intensities of each wave series. But if they don't line up exactly, that is, if their peaks intrude into one another's valleys then a *phase shift* is said to have occurred and the intensity of the intermingled series will be less than the intensity of either one. If the peaks line up perfectly with the valleys and fill them, then the variations in sound pressure cease to exist and the wave series cancel each other out. Such a condition occurs in the case of a 180-degree phase shift (Fig. 3-6). At a 90-degree phase shift, on the other hand, cancellation is partial and incomplete, and sound intensity of the summed wave series is only reduced by half.

Different wave series bear a phase relationship to one another even when they are not the same frequency and when cancellation is not an issue. Suppose, for instance, one takes a musical tone com-

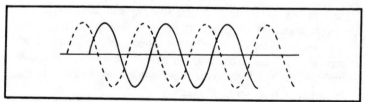

Fig. 3-6. A 180-degree phase shift.

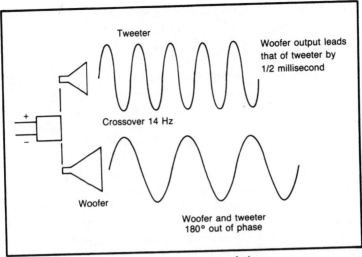

Fig. 3-7. Woofer and tweeter 180 degrees out of phase.

prised of the fundamental Middle C (261.83) and a series of over-tones extending out past the limits of human hearing. Now suppose one takes this complex tone and sends it through an electronic filter set at 300 Hz where frequencies above 300 Hz are routed through one circuit and those below 300 Hz are sent through another. Just such a process occurs in most loudspeakers in which the woofer, or low frequency element, gets one set of frequencies and the tweeter, the high frequency element, gets another (Fig. 3-7). Such filters inevitably change the phase relationship of high and low frequencies, causing the highs to lead or lag the lows by a tiny fraction of a second. The precise duration of the time lag is not uniform but varies between tones of different frequencies. Such variable time delay caused by electronic filters is known as *group delay* or sometimes *envelope distortion* because the shape or envelope of a complex wave form becomes grossly altered. As we shall see, envelope distortion is very much an issue in digital recording.

ELECTRONIC MEASUREMENTS

The three terms frequency, intensity, and phase give the vocabulary for fully describing any sound and thus for assessing the performance of any audio component. However, except for a loudspeaker, no audio component, including a compact disc player, produces sound directly. All other audio components pass signals which are electrical analogs of sound waves, and a somewhat more extensive vocabulary must be devised for assessing electrical performance because the behavior of electrons flowing through a circuit is not an exact analog of sound waves traveling through air. Because the analogy between electron flow and acoustical phenomena is at the heart of audio electronics, it merits discussion.

Electrons, as most of us recall, are negatively charged subatomic particles that repel one another, but are attracted to positively charged objects, namely those with relative absence of electrons within the orbits of the atoms comprising those objects. In a sense, electrons behave similarly to air molecules in that they migrate away from areas of high pressure where they are abundant into areas of low pressure where they are scarce.

The flow of electrons in an electrical circuit from a high pressure, negatively charged pole to a low pressure, positively charged pole can be regulated so as to form pulses—spurts of electrons under high pressure followed by lulls where few electrons flow and pressure in the circuit is low. (The term for electrical pressure is *voltage*.) The nomenclature for such regulation when it is accomplished by sound waves acting on some electromechanical device is *transduction*. Transduction, generally, refers to the conversion of one form of energy to another. An example of such transduction occurs in a dynamic microphone when sound waves strike the diaphragm which itself is attached to a coil of thin wire. The sound moves the diaphragm which, in turn, moves the coil within a powerful magnetic field. The movement of the coil within the magnetic field generates an electrical voltage just as in an electrical dynamo. The resulting spurt of electrons follows pretty closely the form of the sound waves moving the diaphragm. This spurt of electrons can then be used to power a motor consisting of a reverse arrangement of coils and magnets that can ultimately be used to move another diaphragm to recreate the original sound. That is essentially what happens in a telephone (Fig. 3-8).

In consumer audio systems, this type of analog electronic technology was all pervasive until very recently. The Compact Disc in particular and digital recording in general represent an alternative method for storing and transmitting audio information electronically, a method which, in time, is likely to make obsolete much of the older analog technology. But for the time being, most of the processing of an electrical signal that occurs in a consumer audio system takes place in the analog domain. The Compact Disc Player itself contains a multitude of analog circuits and its output is an analog signal. The performance of these analog circuits turns out to be crucial to the ultimate performance of the players, and these analog circuits are also the area of the players where the greatest differences in design and performance occur.

Before I describe how the performance of analog circuits is specified, one further element should be examined in these circuits—namely, the audio amplifier.

We mentioned earlier that the electrical energy generated by a transducer could be used to power a motor assembly for a sound producing diaphragm or loudspeaker. Early telephones worked on this principle with nothing but a length of wire between the front end transducer into which one party spoke and the terminal transducer over which the other party listened. The problems with such a simple approach are that the electrical resistance of the connecting wire weakens the signal over distance, and the voltage from the front end transducer is so low to begin with that a full sized loudspeaker can't be used for a terminal transducer. There just isn't enough electrical power.

Fortunately, an electrical audio signal can be boosted without much loss of information by a device called an audio amplifier; this takes the original signal from the front end transducer whether it be a microphone, phonograph, or whatever, and uses it to control a circuit that functions as a valve or gate and regulates the flow of a higher voltage stream of electrons from a power supply in response to the fluctuations of the original signal. In this manner, a larger, stronger replica of the original signal is created—one that can drive a loudspeaker. Most modern audio amplifiers use tran-

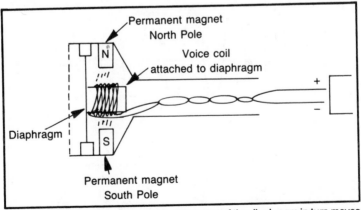

Fig. 3-8. With a dynamic microphone, movement of the diaphragm in turn moves the voice coil in the magnetic gap, and generates the flow of electrons through the voice coil.

43

sistors to perform the role of valves, although until the mid 1960s vacuum tubes were more commonly employed in this function.

Audio amplifiers are not perfect and they characteristically introduce unwanted additions to an audio signal known as *distortion* (Fig. 3-9). Such distortion takes three basic forms: *harmonic, enharmonic,* and *intermodulation. Harmonic distortion* is the production of a series of frequencies spaced at octave intervals above the frequency being reproduced by the amplifier. These correspond to the harmonics produced by musical instruments except that in the case of most musical instruments, harmonics diminish in intensity with ascending frequency whereas with most modern audio amplifiers the opposite is true—that is, the higher pitched harmonics grow more intense than the lower order harmonics. Because harmonics grow more audible and more irritating as one ascends the musical scale, the distortion characteristics of most modern amplifiers are extremely undesirable (the older vacuum tube amplifiers produced most of their distortion in the form of relatively innocuous low order distortions with steadily diminishing quantities of upper octave distortion).

Harmonic distortion, overall, is listed as a percentage of total signal strength. The usual term used in current specifications is total harmonic distortion, THD, which is the sum of all of the spurious harmonics generated by the amplifier. In most present day amplifiers that percentage is a fraction of 1 percent with most of the distortion being of the high order upper octave variety. The

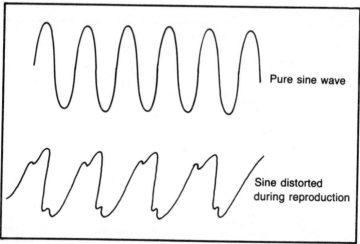

Pure sine wave

Sine distorted during reproduction

Fig. 3-9. Examples of distortion.

audibility of these distortions in such low quantities is debatable. Certainly such distortions are present in the circuits of compact disc players and will be discussed further.

Enharmonic distortions, distortions unrelated by regular intervals to the frequency of the signal, may also be generated by audio amplifiers and are extremely unpleasant sounding even at very low values. Enharmonic distortion is almost never listed in audio specifications although it can be measured.

Intermodulation distortion might be construed as a form of enharmonic distortion although it's certainly not the only such form. Intermodulation distortion or IM as it's called for short, consists of what is known as sum and difference tones that are produced when an amplifier receives an input of two tones simultaneously. The difference tone is just that, the difference between the higher and lower frequencies. If, for instance, an amplifier is given an input signal consisting of a sine wave of 40 Hz and another of 400 Hz, a difference tone of 360 Hz will be generated. Conversely, the sum tone of the same two tones is 440 Hz.

Intermodulation distortion, also known as *Doppler distortion*, is also a problem in loudspeakers and is easier to visualize in a mechanical system such as a loudspeaker cone. If the cone is making large low frequency back and forth motions while simultaneously attempting to reproduce higher pitched tones, the low frequency motions will, in effect, raise and lower the pitch of the higher pitched tone (Fig. 3-10). The analog, usually given for Doppler distortion is a train whistle that rises in pitch as the train approaches, and falls as the train passes. Something similar can

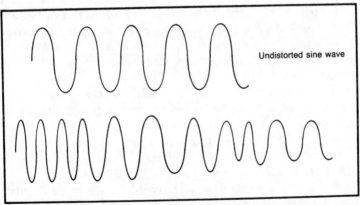

Fig. 3-10. Sine waves being modulated by a lower frequency. Note how wave peaks get closer together and then further apart.

happen in an amplifier amplifying multiple tones simultaneously, although most amplifiers produce considerably less IM than loudspeakers do. IM is a particularly annoying type of distortion and is generally present instead of harmonic distortion in higher values with electronic components. Many engineers theorize that high values of IM are the chief cause of audible problems in electronic amplifiers. In any case, IM specifications are seldom provided by the manufacturers of either loudspeakers or amplifiers. IM, like THD, is listed as a percentage of total signal strength, and values of well under 1 percent are desirable.

A special kind of intermodulation distortion began to receive attention a few years ago known as *transient intermodulation distortion* or TIM. TIM is a condition occurring when an amplifying circuit receives a brief, powerful high frequency signal and momentarily overloads as a result. TIM is a transient phenomenon associated with rapidly changing signals with pronounced high frequency content, and it does not show up in standard distortion tests. No generally accepted method for testing TIM has ever been devised and, as a consequence, it is seldom listed in factory specifications for a component.

Wow, Flutter, and Microphonics

In addition to generating distortion, all consumer audio playback systems suffer from two other anomalies that detract from the realism of reproduced sound—speed inconstancy and microphonics.

Speed inconstancy is a mechanical malfunction rather than a problem in the circuitry. It occurs by virtue of the fact that all audio playback systems on the market utilize media that are exposed to the playback device progressively, one area at a time on a continuous basis. Thus, tape is wound past a magnetic playback head, a phonograph record is spun beneath a movable phonograph stylus, and a compact disc is spun in a similar manner beneath a laser pickup. All of these media depend for their proper functioning on the transport—that is, the motor which is moving the storage medium past the pickup—providing said movement at a closely regulated rate of speed. Any significant deviation from set speed will cause problems in reproduction.

In an analog turntable or tape recorder, such speed fluctuating will induce variations in pitch, heard as a kind of vibrato or sourness in sustained notes and a general blurring and smearing of complex instrumental passages and percussive transients. In analog systems, speed inconstancy is a matter of degree. Virtually any measurable speed inconstancy degrades the sound, but quite a bit is required before it really becomes objectionable. In digital systems, as we shall explain in some detail in the following chapter, speed inconstancy either has no effect at all or causes a total loss of information. That's because digital systems contain provisions for making the digital storage of audio information largely independent of the speed of the transport—up to a point. Beyond that point, disaster threatens. As with so many other aspects of digital sound, speed constancy is an all or nothing matter.

The common specification for speed inconstancy is wow and flutter, *wow* referring to low frequency speed variations that actually impart a vibrato to the sound, and *flutter* to high speed variations that tend to make tones sound off pitch and distorted, and that seem to interfere with the reproduction of ambience cues in a recording. Wow and flutter are usually lumped together in a single measurement despite the fact that they are subjectively different, and that wow is generally less deleterious to musical reproduction. A figure of 0.1 percent speed deviation for combined wow and flutter has long been considered acceptable performance for an analog turntable. In contrast, the compact disc format specifies wow and flutter that is essentially immeasurable.

Much controversy surrounds the issue of wow and flutter, with many audiophiles contending that the 0.1 percent standard is inadequate. From about 1975 onward, increasing numbers of audiophiles invested in beltdrive turntables with massive, precisely balanced platters by such manufacturers as Linn, SOTA, Micro Seiki, and Oracle on the theory that the high moment of inertia provided by such platters insured an extreme immunity to high frequency pitch variation and, consequently, much enhanced reproduction. Such claims are difficult to prove in scientific blind listening tests, but they have been widely accepted by serious listeners and they would tend to suggest that the compact disc format's exceptionally tight speed regulation is anything but overkill.

Microphonics, the other anomaly we mentioned, is virtually never specified directly. Microphonics refers to acoustic feedback, the situation occurring when sound waves from the loudspeakers disturb some other component in the audio chain. Turntables are notoriously subject to microphonics, and so are old fashioned vacuum tube amplifiers. Some evidence exists to the effect that transistors are mildly microphonic (some Japanese manufacturers

47

actually soundproof their amplifier cabinets) as well as compact disc player transports. Sound waves vibrating the platter that rotates the compact disc may actually cause it to mistrack. I know of no measurement to indicate the propensity of players to mistrack when exposed to high playback levels, although I suspect mistracking will occur. It certainly does with phonograph records in which tracking isn't nearly as precise. However, in the case of compact discs, error correction circuits will tend to mask mistracking unless it is extraordinarily severe.

INTERPRETING SPECIFICATIONS

Audio specifications are meaningless to the consumer unless they can be correlated to observable phenomenon, specifically differences in the audible performance of audio components. If differences in specifications fail to relate to differences in audible performance, or if audible performance varies in a way that standard specifications fail to indicate, then the consumer has a problem. The latter seems to be the case with the compact disc format.

The compact disc format was designed in such a manner that it would offer measured performance that is superior by an order of magnitude over that of the phonograph record. At the same time, basic design considerations dictated a lack of significant differences in measured performance among the different models of compact disc players.

The consumer who focuses on standard specifications alone can only conclude that compared to the compact disc player, all phonographs are hopelessly lacking in fidelity, and that compact disc players all sound the same and are all essentially perfect. Preoccupation with standard specifications has in fact led to numerous statements in the press to the effect that the worst compact disc player outperforms the best phonograph by a wide margin and that within the compact disc player category all players perform at the same level.

Before anyone can begin to address such statements he must first examine the meaning of standard specifications in terms of real world performance. The rest of this chapter is devoted to the topic of how the two really relate to one another.

The first specification generally considered in discussing any audio medium is its frequency range, that is, the span of frequencies that it can reproduce. Human beings are commonly said to be able to hear from 15-20 Hz to 20 kHz, and, therefore, a range approaching those limits is considered to be desirable in a high fidelity medium (Fig. 3-11).

The compact disc, in fact, has a frequency range extending from 20 Hz out to 20 kHz exactly. The bandwidth is very sharply defined, and within this bandwidth the response of most machines should not vary more than a decibel or so for any frequency. Frequency response can thus be considered good to excellent.

In contrast to the compact disc, the phonograph record has vaguely defined limits for its frequency response. A phonograph record may contain low level information out to about 80 kHz in the treble, and may extend to as low as 8 Hz in the bass though a recording lacquer is difficult to cut at frequencies lower than 30 Hz. Most phonograph records, in fact, have little response above 20 kHz and older stereo records have negligable response above 15 kHz.

The compact disc is generally conceded to have an advantage over the phonograph in the bass while it clearly has less high frequency extension than the best phonograph records. But what does all this really mean in terms of listening impressions? If human hearing extends only from 20 Hz to 20 kHz, aren't they about equivalent in frequency range?

Not precisely. Recent research has indicated that many humans can hear overtones, though not pure tones, extending considerably beyond 20 kHz, and that such overtones play a role in both the localization of sounds and the definition of the distinctive tonal qualities associated with individual musical instruments. In this light, the 20 kHz upper limit of the compact disc does constitute a limitation.

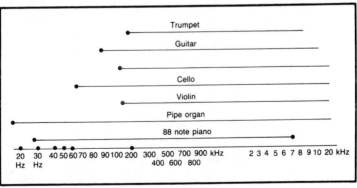

Fig. 3-11. The frequency ranges of some common musical instruments. Overtones are included.

So why not make it higher—say 100 kHz? A higher bandwidth might be possible with present day digital circuitry, but in the late 1970s, when the current compact disc standards were formulated, 20 kHz constituted a practical upper limit. Even an additional octave of bandwidth which would have dictated a 40 kHz limit, was not feasible.

Dynamic Range

Beyond frequency response, dynamic range is always cited as a key specification in discussing any high fidelity medium, and here the compact disc is most impressive. The standard specification for the dynamic range of the compact disc format is over 90 dB. Assuming that the lowest level audible sound that a compact disc-based system would reproduce would be about 40 dB (few domestic environments have background noise levels of under 40 dB, therefore, background noise will tend to drown out sounds below that level), the system would, at its loudest, crank out sounds at an ear-shattering 130 dB.

However, such dynamic range is more a theoretical limit than a practical possibility. The compact disc player may, in fact, deliver at output a spread of voltages encompassing a 90 dB dynamic range (electrical flow, like sound pressure, can be measured in decibels, and a direct relationship exists in an audio system between decibel increases in electrical flow at source output and decibel increases in actual sound pressure at the loudspeaker level). This electrical output from the compact disc player certainly has the potential for producing a similar range in variation of sound pressure levels; however, to produce the full range of variations, very abundant amplifier power is required and equally abundant power handling capability will be required in the loudspeakers.

Assuming a base level of 40 dB above the threshold of hearing and a peak level of 130 dB, one would be hard put to span the entire dynamic range of the compact disc with any currently available consumer audio speaker system. The most efficient consumer speaker system made, the Klipschorn, has an upper limit of 125 dB and requires 128 watts to reach that level (Fig. 3-12). Sustained 130 dB levels would damage the speakers and would require about 400 watts per channel, which exceeds the capabilities of all but a handful of power amps on the market. In other words, a combination of the most efficient speakers and the most powerful amplifiers will not yield 130 dB sound pressure levels, so in practical

Fig. 3-12. A Klipschorn speaker.

terms, the full dynamic range of the compact disc is simply not available in the home. Furthermore, regardless of the hoopla from manufacturers concerning new "digital-ready" loudspeakers, the principles of loudspeaker design have not changed fundamentally since the advent of the compact disc and there is little evidence that speakers as a whole have significantly increased either power handling or efficiency. That is because increasing either power handling or efficiency generally involves trade-offs in accuracy and freedom from distortion and this isn't likely to change. Typically, quality component home audio systems have maximum sound pressure levels in the 105 dB range. Thus, the actual dynamic range available to most consumers from the compact disc format is about 65 dB.

How does this compare with the dynamic range of the phonograph? Dynamic range figures given for phonograph records vary from 50 to about 65 or 70 dB. Records encoded by the dbx process may have more than 80 dB dynamic range, but unencoded records certainly have much less, and 50 dB is probably nearer to the truth than 65 dB. A 65 dB dynamic range is probably within the physical capabilities of the medium, but would require groove widths which few record cutting engineers would countenance, and would also necessitate very quiet, high quality vinyl. So in essence, the useful dynamic range of either medium is not that different.

Phase Response

This is the one area in which at least some CD players tend to look bad on paper compared to the phonograph and where they differ markedly from one another.

A phonograph record itself is pretty linear in regard to phase. Most phonograph cartridges are not. The cantilever of a phono cartridge generally resonates at anywhere from 10 kHz to 30 kHz. This resonance creates considerable phase shift in the top octave. A couple of cartridges, notably the Dynavector Diamond and the Win FET have resonant frequencies much higher—in the 100 kHz range. They do not exhibit much phase shift in the audible range.

Compact disc players with analog filters usually have hundreds of degrees of phase shift in the top octave. The audible effects of this phase shift are debatable, but evidence is growing that it effects the stereo imaging of an audio system and its ability to reproduce instrumental timbres. Players using digital filters and the four times oversampling system described in Chapter 4 show only a few degrees of phase shift in the audible frequency range. However digital mastering itself usually introduces a lot of phase shift that is not generally corrected for by oversampling players, so the total phase shift of the medium is still apt to be quite high.

Distortion

Distortion specifications for compact disc players are most impressive also. The majority of players rate at less than 0.05 percent total harmonic distortion which is negligable by most standards. Phonographs are difficult to compare in this respect because phonograph records themselves vary considerably in the degrees to which they distort the signals fed into the record cutting lathers, but THD for the record itself may approach 5 percent plus another half or one percent from the phono cartridge on playback. In other words, distortion is apt to be hundreds of times higher than that of the compact disc medium, which isn't even including IM and unharmonic sideband phenomena for the phonograph record. With half speed mastering and high quality playback equipment, phonograph distortion figures can be brought down to less than 1 percent, but this is hardly the norm.

What are we to make of these figures? Distortions in the medium of the phonograph record are certainly high enough to be audible. Even records cut from the best vinyl with absolutely the lowest amounts of surface noise exhibit tonal quality that is subtly different from that of a master tape. In this matter of distortion, the compact disc seems decisively superior to the phonograph record, but again the issue is not so simple as it first appears.

First of all, digital recording, in general, may be prone to quite high degrees of subharmonic distortions, that is, distortion products at frequencies below those of the musical tones being recorded and, hence, not apparent in the readings of conventional distortion analyzers. Several researchers, including Keith Johnson, inventor of the focus gap tape recorder, have reported such subharmonic distortion, and Johnson has suggested methods for reducing it. The existence of these subharmonics has generally not been acknowledged in the industry at large and, in any case, they are a product of the digital mastering process and not compact disc playback; they won't show up in the specs, although they may be audible.

The other respect in which the compact disc and other digital recording media compare unfavorably with the older analog media as regards distortion is that, distortions in digital media typically increase with falling signal level, while in analog media the opposite is true. Digital sound sources, including the compact disc, are measured for distortion at their maximum signal strength as has been traditionally done with analog sources. The comparison in that respect is hardly fair, particularly when one considers that early digital recording techniques produced distortion approaching 100 percent at the lowest level. Present day digital audio devices perform much better in this respect, and harmonic distortion is pretty well controlled down to the lowest levels, but it does still increase with falling signal strength.

Finally, it should be noted that the distortions in the analog phonograph record, while relatively quite high, are predominetly second and third harmonics and are not especially audible or offensive. Analog phonograph records look very bad on paper compared to digital media or high quality analog tape recorders, and yet when played back on very high resolution phonograph systems, records can yield startlingly realistic reproductions of sound.

Noise

Compact discs and compact disc players, unless malfunctioning, are dead quiet. Noise figures are similar to those for dynamic range, better than 90 dB, and noise won't increase with repeated playings provided discs are not abused. There is no question that the noiseless quality of compact discs is one of their major selling points. Compared to most recordings on black vinyl, the CD versions sound razor sharp and incredibly clean.

Nevertheless, in this, as in other specifications, all is not as it seems. The digital recording process imposes rigid limits in every performance parameter, frequency range dynamic range, distortion and so forth. The codes employed on the disc can hold only so much information and no more, and faced with the task of encoding information beyond the limits of the code, they fail dramatically. In contrast, when unencoded analog recording media are overloaded or pushed beyond their limits they simply show a gradually increasing inability to handle the signal. In other words, their limits are not sharply defined.

So what does this have to do with noise? Only that the phonograph record as a recording medium is endowed with the ability to capture sounds considerably below its own noise floor, perhaps 10 dB lower in intensity that the noise itself. Digital recording has no such capability and many music critics and recording engineers have complained of digital recorders "going deaf" at low levels—failing to record the faint reverberation in a symphony or the long decay of a struck piano string. For many, this deafness, this collision of the medium with its own noise limit, is its most obvious failing.

Separation

Separation is a specification relating to the relative independence of two stereo signals, that is, the degree to which they remain isolated within a given component. Ideally, separation should be infinite—no leakage should occur between left and right channels, and in compact disc players, separation is infinite for all practical purposes. In phonograph systems, on the other hand, leakage from opposite channels, termed crosstalk in audio parlance, will in most cases be about 35 dB below signal level and often no better than 20 dB below signal level.

Here again, the compact disc appears far superior on paper, but the superiority is not so readily apparent in actual listening. A separation figure of 20 dB appears to be quite adequate to produce a good sense of left and right in a stereo presentation, and infinite separation, while theoretically desirable, is not practically necessary. It is doubtful that most listeners could distinguish between infinite separation and 40 dB separation, and as we have seen, some phono cartridges can approach the 40 dB figure.

SPECIFICATIONS IN INDIVIDUAL PLAYERS

The consumer will note when shopping for a compact disc player and comparing specifications from manufacturers as well as those listed in test reports that the players all spec out pretty much alike in terms of THD, dynamic range, noise, and channel separation. One doesn't seem to get enhanced performance for greater expenditures. A really diligent or curious consumer will find that the same situation applies to most other audio components, tuners, receivers, amplifiers, turntables and phono cartridges. The standard specifications generally don't differ much among components in a given category. The mass market audio publications generally take this uniformity in standard specifications to mean uniform performance regardless of price level. My own position is that standard specifications provide an incomplete picture of performance and that manufacturers tend to optimize performance to meet standard specifications and neglect other criteria. Since nonstandard specifications are generally not supplied, the consumer has to learn to educate his own ears and also to look for circuit topologies and construction quality that are of demonstrable sonic merit. Well-engineered compact disc players do cost more to produce than underengineered models, although cost and quality don't always have a one to one relationship. Chapter 7 contains a detailed discussion on the variations in design that really make a difference in sound.

Chapter 4

Fundamentals of Digital
Recording and Playback

Briefly touched upon in Chapter 1 were the differences between
analog and digital signals. Analog signals, you may recall, are continuous, infinitely variable streams of information in the form of
rounded waves. Digital signals, on the other hand, are series of discrete pulses or packets of information. A digital system has two
states—not an infinite number of states—and those two states are
"on" and "off."

Sound, itself, is an analog phenomenon. Both frequency and
amplitude are infinitely variable, and, thus analog electrical audio
recording is a much more direct mode of storing audio information
than is digital recording (though that doesn't necessarily make analog recording superior). In an analog phonograph record the ripples in the groove walls pretty exactly follow the form of the sound
waves traveling through the air. The short ripples are high frequencies, the long ripples are low frequencies, the deeper ripples are
loud sounds, and the shallow ripples are soft sounds. The groove
is almost a print of the sound wave, and in the case of direct-to-
disk recording, it may be a very direct print, with sound waves strik-
ing a microphone and producing electrical currents, and these currents then going into an amplifier that, in turn, drives a record cutter
which finally scratches the wave form into the lacquer master (Fig.
4-1).

Digital recording is both less direct and far more complex. Digital recordings start the same way as their analog counterparts.

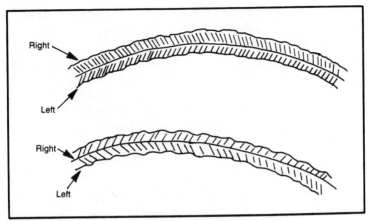

Fig. 4-1. Phonograph record grooves.

Sound waves strike a microphone diaphragm whose movements generate a flow of electrons. The weak electrical flow from the microphone is amplified, and the boosted electrical signal is then fed into the recording device.

But from there on, the two processes diverge sharply. Instead of being used to regulate a larger current flow of a similar wave form, the analog signal in the digital recording device is used to activate a series of electronic switches which produce binary numbers that correspond to the voltage of the signal at discrete intervals of time. These binary numbers produced at a rate of 44.1 times per second in the compact disc format, constitute the digital code for the initial analog audio signal.

Eventually, the encoded information is converted back into an analog audio signal, but not before being re-encoded several times. The re-encoding is done to facilitate the storage of the information within a physical medium of very restricted size, to protect the information from losses occurring in transmission, and to detect such losses when they do occur. Once encoded, the digitized audio information can be stored almost indefinitely. When it is to be called up and played back as sound, separate circuits decode the digital information, and a set of electronic switches releases varying intensities of electrical current that correspond more or less exactly to the varying electrical voltages that were recorded at input. However, this output contains a large component of high frequency distortion imparted by the set of electronic switches that was employed to produce an analog signal from the digital code, and this distortion must be removed by an electronic filter or filters at the final stage. From there, the signal is ready for amplification and playback through a conventional audio system (Fig. 4-2).

In the following sections, we will describe the complete process of digital recording and playback beginning with the actual performance and ending with the generation of an analog signal at the output of a compact disc player. It will be understood, of course, that the recording takes place entirely in the production of the compact disc. Compact disc players themselves have no provisions for recording sounds and contain no recording circuitry.

INPUT

A digital recording begins with a musical performance. The actual process of picking up the sounds of the recording with a microphone and then transmitting the electrical impulses generated by the microphone preamplifier to the tape recorder are no different in digital recording from its analog counterpart. The tape recorders themselves differ markedly, however, as do the tape formulations used in them. The special characteristics of digital tape recording heads and tape types are beyond the scope of this book, but the digital encoding circuits that are used to change the audio signal into digital form are very apropos to our discussion of compact discs since they constitute the ultimate source of the digitized information that is recovered by the compact disc player. All compact discs begin with a digital tape recording. In some cases, that recording has been transferred from an analog master, but there must be a digitized tape recording somewhere in the recording process because a compact disc cutting lathe will *not accept an analog audio signal.*

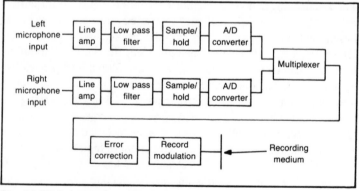

Fig. 4-2. Digital recording signal path.

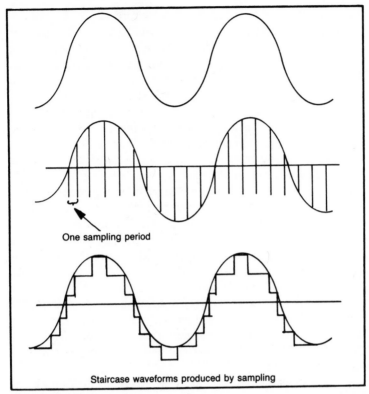

One sampling period

Staircase waveforms produced by sampling

Fig. 4-3. Staircase waveforms.

SAMPLING

The heart of a digital recording is a process known as *sampling*. Sampling in this application means just what it appears to mean—taking a succession of samples. The samples taken here are samples of the audio wave forms one is attempting to record.

The word sample generally implies a limited but representative quantity of a whole, and that is precisely what it implies here. In analog recording, at least in theory, the whole and entire audio wave form is impressed on the recording medium. In digital recording, only certain dimensions of the waveforms are actually recorded (Fig. 4-3).

On this account, digital recording may seem disturbingly sketchy, but theoretically sufficient information is recorded to reconstruct the original analog waveform precisely. To understand why the sampling process enables the digital recording medium to preserve sufficient information to reproduce sounds accurately, you must go back to the discussion of the nature of sound waves.

As you may recall from the third chapter, all sounds, however complex, can be broken down into successions of sine waves that vary both in frequency and intensity in naturally occurring sounds. A sine or sinusoidal wave is a very precise alteration in air pressure with fixed duration, intensity, and shape. Provided that one can obtain both high and low-pressure readings for a given cycle of a sine wave, one can deduce the slope of the wave since the slope is invariable and always describes the same curve. To record any sine wave, only two bits of information are required: the high pressure reading or peak, and the low pressure reading or trough. It doesn't hurt to have readings on intermediate pressure levels, but they are not absolutely required to reconstitute the slope.

To get both the high and low pressure readings for a single cycle of a sine wave, that wave must be sampled twice during a single cycle. Thus, if one is sampling a sine wave that has a frequency of 100 Hz, that wave must be sampled at a rate of 200 Hz or 200 times per second. To sample a waveform at the conventional limits of human hearing at 20 kHz, a sampling rate of some 40,000 times per second must be used minimally. The 44.1 kHz sampling rate used in the compact disc medium is just slightly above the minimum required for 20 kHz tones, and provides a margin of safety, a guard band as it were.

A Danish mathematician named Sven Nyquist devised a theorum bearing his name, proving that a sampling rate of double the highest recorded frequency was sufficient for the perfect reproduction of sine waves of the highest recorded frequency, and of any frequencies below that point. Thus, the sampling rate used in a digital recording system is often referred to as the *Nyquist limit*.

You will recall the mention earlier that digital recording systems require considerably more bandwidth than analog systems to record audio waveforms of the same frequencies. In fact, the theoretical lower limit of a digital system is only twice the recorded frequency, but due to other factors, the actual bandwidths of all existing digital recording systems, including the compact disc, are several octaves above the stated sampling rate. The total bandwidth for the compact disc format is nearly one megahertz.

RESOLUTION AND BIT RATE

If sampling rate determines the bandwidth of a digital recording system, bit count determines the dynamic range of that same system.

As indicated earlier in the text, digital encoding of audio frequencies has much in common with information storage in a digital computer, and the term *bit* has precisely the same meaning it has in computer terminology, namely, the smallest unit of information, or—to put it another way—a single digit in a numerical code. As do all modern digital computers, digital recorders use numerical codes written in the binary number system based on the number two instead of ten. This number system contains only two numbers, 1 and 0. 1 and 0 each represent one bit. We will not dwell upon a lengthy review of the binary number system here. Suffice it to say that in binary notation each addition of two units will be represented by a power of ten. Thus, $1 + 1 = 10(2); 10 + 1 = 11(3); 11 + 1 = 100(4); 100 + 1 = 101(5)$; etc.

Obviously, the more bits allowable for representing different voltages, the greater the number of discrete voltage levels that may be represented by the code, and the greater the total range of voltages that can be represented, provided, of course, that the numbers are used in a linear code in which each additional digit represents an increase in magnitude on the order of one power.

The 16 bit code used in the compact disc permits a dynamic range in excess of 90 dB and total of 65,536 different intensity levels in between. The bit rate would appear to be more than adequate to encompass the dynamic range of music.

The sampling rate and the bit count are the chief parameters of any digital recording system. Sampling rate determines frequency range or bandwidth, and the bit count determines dynamic range. It's all very cut-and-dried.

FILTERING

Digital recording systems, unlike their analog counterparts, must be used within well-defined limits in both the areas of frequency range and dynamic range. If a digital system is presented with a signal too high pitched for it to sample adequately, it will produce spurious tones known as aliased frequencies that are lower in pitch than the upper limits of the recording system, and which represent parts of the high frequency signal. Like intermodulation distortions, which they resemble, aliased frequencies are completely unrelated to the musical signal and thus stand out as particularly obnoxious forms of musical impurities. To avoid aliasing frequencies, all current digital systems utilize sharp electronic filters that largely preclude high frequencies from entering the system in the first place. These *antialiasing filters* form the first element in the digital recording chain and the filtering process, itself, is the first step in converting the audio signal into digital form.

Digital systems also have problems with sounds that are too low or too loud to be encompassed by the bit rate, or, in other words, with sounds which generate voltages at the microphone level that are either too low to generate consistent readings by the analog-to-digital convertor, or that are too large to be expressed by the available number of bits.

Either situation is sonically disastrous, but professional digital recording systems have bit rates sufficiently high so that they are very seldom overloaded. The real problem lies at the low end, that is, in the recording of very soft sounds.

In analog-to-digital convertors, which we will consider in greater detail later in this chapter, a series of electronic switches, also known as gates, are triggered by the input voltages, with higher voltages activating more gates. The gates, which can only switch on or off, produce the 1s and 0s in the digital numerical code. The gates representing the higher numbers in the code naturally respond to larger voltage swings and the gate controlling the last digit to the right or "least significant bit" responds to very minute voltage swings and must be extremely precise. But when voltages at input drop to a certain predetermined point, they will fail to trigger the gate for the least significant bit in a consistent manner, and, instead, they will activate the gate at odd intervals, and will produce a whole spectrum of tones unrelated to the musical signal. Such spurious tones are known as *quantization noise* or *granulation noise* and cannot be eliminated by the input filters used in digital recording systems simply because this noise occurs after the filtering as part of the digital conversion itself.

DITHER

Granulation noise is combatted by means of a process known as dithering (not related in any sense to the agreeable process of wasting time or puttering about ineffectually). A *dither* is a device for generating a small quantity of noise—noise which is fed into the input of the digital recorder along with the signal on a continuous basis. Dither ensures that the gate controlling the least significant bit is always activated and prevents the production of granulation noise. In a sense, it is a form of biasing.

The idea of injecting noise into a system to improve its performance may seem a bit bizarre, especially in view of the efforts analog circuit designers expend on reducing noise in their circuits, but, there is no question that the cure is better than the disease even though dither slightly reduces effective dynamic range and signal-to-noise ratio. It might be added that ordinary white noise serves well for dithering and is commonly employed, though other types of tone combinations have been used as well.

The dither generator, or dither for short, actually precedes the antialiasing filter because, as we have seen, the filter itself is power-less to deal with granulation noise. The dither generator is not ac-tually part of the signal path in the recording chain, but it performs an indispensable function.

ANALOG-TO-DIGITAL CONVERSION

Once low-pass filtered, and dithered, the analog signal is then ready for its conversion into a digital code, the point at which digi-tal audio, as such, actually begins.

The first stage in this process is sampling and is performed within what is known as a *sample and hold circuit*. A sample and hold circuit is a fairly simple device consisting of an electronic switch, a quartz oscillator for opening and closing the switch at a specified rate, and a buffer subcircuit for matching the electrical impedance of the sample and hold circuit to that of the following stage.

The oscillator in the sample and hold circuit is set at the sam-pling rate to be used for recording so, in the case of a professional digital audio tape recorder, the switch opens once every 1/48,000 of a second. The oscillator must be highly accurate, for any sig-nificant variation in sampling will cause audible distortion in the high frequencies. When the oscillator opens the switch, the analog signal (generally taken from a microphone feed) flows through the switch for as long as the switch remains open, which must be for a tiny increment of the total sampling time. The switch closes and opens again one sampling cycle later.

The electrical current flowing through the switch charges up a component known as a *capacitor*. A capacitor is an electrode with positive and negative terminals separated by a bit of electrically resistive material—an open circuit so to speak. If the oscillator and switch do the sampling, the capacitor does the holding (Fig. 4-4).

A capacitor, when it is presented with an alternating electrical current, retards the flow of that current for a certain interval of time which depends on the electrical value of the capacitor. The capacitor is said to charge and discharge, that is, accept and release an electrical charge. During the discharge process the voltage of the capacitor falls until it returns to the original level it held before the capacitor was charged. The time required for the capacitor to discharge will depend upon the intensity of the charge, in other words, the voltage. This quality of capacitors to vary discharge times according to voltage, is frequently exploited in the following stage of a digital recorder, the actual digital-to-analog convertor.

There are two principal ways, described below, of designing an analog to digital convertor, but both such convertors perform essentially the same function, that is, they measure the voltage of the charge in the capacitor contained within the sample and hold circuit, and assign a digital number to that measurement.

The most basic method for performing this conversion is known as *successive approximation*. To understand successive approximation one must keep in mind that each bit in the code used for storing the audio signal in digital form stands for a single unit within a digital number in the binary system, and that each unit in the number is a power of two smaller than the number preceding it. The first digit in the number series is the largest, and each number following is progressively smaller.

Before an explanation is given for exactly how successive approximation is performed, it might be well to say a few words concerning digital encoding schemes in general. In the first chapter I touched upon the subject of modulation which in electronics refers to the imposition of a signal onto a carrier frequency that is always much higher than the highest frequency in the signal itself. I further touched upon the pulse parameter modulation schemes, iden-

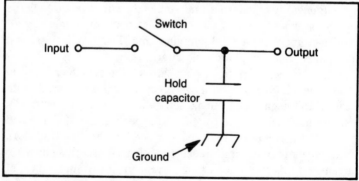

Fig. 4-4. Idealized sample and hold circuit.

tified as essentially digital by virtue of the fact that they made use of discontinuous signals. Pulse parameter encoding systems include *pulse amplitude modulation* in which the amplitude of the pulse is infinitely variable, *pulse position modulation* in which the cadence of the pulses varies, *pulse width modulation* in which the width of the pulses is infinitely variable, *pulse number modulation* in which the pulses are grouped together in sets with varying numbers of pulses, and finally, *pulse code modulation* in which the pulses are assigned bit values and form parts of binary numbers (Fig. 4-5). Those pulse modulation schemes with infinitely variable values along one dimension are actually hybrid systems, analog in one respect, digital in another. None of the hybrid systems offers the measure of fidelity that the two fully digital systems, pulse number modulation and pulse code modulation, do. I mention them primarily because one such system, pulse width modulation, is employed in a type of audio amplifier that is likely to be increasingly employed in the future, especially in conjunction with compact disc players. Pulse code modulation, of course, is the encoding system used with the compact disc and all digital type recorders.

In the successive approximation encoding process the input voltage is arbitrarily assigned the binary number 1,000,000,000,000,000 initially. This number is then converted back into an analog signal in a digital-to-analog convertor (described in

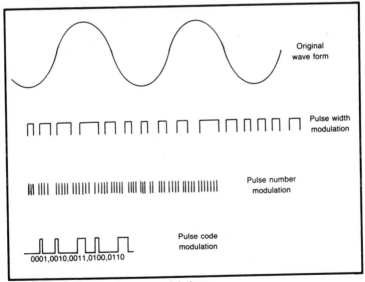

Fig. 4-5. Waveform and pulse modulations.

detail later in this chapter) at an appropriate voltage: that voltage is compared to the input voltage in a comparator circuit. If they match perfectly—a 1 in 65,536 chance in a 16-bit system—the process stops right there; if they don't, it continues.

If the input voltage is larger than the first number, a 1 is entered for the first bit, prior to the next stage of the comparison. If the input voltage is less than the reference voltage signified by the number 1,000,000,000,000,000, then a 0 is entered for the first bit and then the comparison begins anew. The process continues digit by digit until a perfect match is achieved between the input voltage and the voltage produced by the D/A convertor or until the last digit has been reached. The last digit, of course, represents the limits of the system's resolution.

In a 16 bit system, a total of sixteen comparisons may be made for a single sample—all in 1/48,000 of a second. Very high speed circuits and a very accurate D/A convertor are required for this scheme to produce accurate results.

Successive approximation A/D convertors are still used in some PCM modules, but they have largely been supplanted by a second type known as an *integrated convertor*. Integrated convertors operate by measuring the duration that elapses between the time the capacitor in the sample and hold circuit is charged with the sample and the time that the capacitor has discharged completely and reached a zero voltage reading. As has been seen, the higher the voltage the more time must elapse; the relationship between voltage and elapsed time is quite linear.

The measurement is done by a digital counter or clock circuit in tandem with a comparator circuit. The comparator circuit compares the output of the capacitor with a zero reference voltage. When the two coincide, the comparator shuts off the clock. At this point, the clock produces a digital number and that is the value of the sample.

For 16 bit resolution, the clock must be able to measure increments of time equivalent to 3.17 to the -10 power of a second. This, in turn, requires a clock rate in the 3 gigahertz range. Circuits of such speed are difficult to design, and virtually all integrating convertors in use today use slower clock speeds. In order to avoid sacrificing resolution they use two clocks each of 8 bits resolution. The second counter is faster than the first, 256 times as fast to be exact, and it supplies an extra degree of resolution. When the first clock reaches its final bit which is a tiny fraction of the output voltage of the capacitor, 1/256, in fact, it is clocked by the second counter which then proceeds to count in very fine gradations of time. The resolution and accuracy of this dual slope step integration scheme is equal to that of the single integration system, and yet it requires a bandwidth of only 50 MegaHertz for the whole operation.

MULTIPLEXING

Following the conversion of the analog sample into a digital word, the information in the digital word is serialized, that is, it is expressed in a single stream of information with one bit following another.

As indicated, the number initially takes the form of the combined outputs of a number of digital switching circuits passing current simultaneously—or in parallel—to use the proper electronics term. Multiple parallel signals are difficult to store—remember four-channel sound—but, fortunately, digital circuitry provides an easy solution to that problem. The parallel signals can be successively fed into a single serial stream of information occupying a single channel with theoretically no loss of information. Separate bits apart from those representing the audio signal itself are used to indicate the beginning and end of each 16-bit string used to represent each individual sample.

The output of an A/D convertor is parallel data, with one channel assigned per bit; a circuit called a multiplexer is used to render the output into serial form and to assign it all to a single channel. This multiplexing operation is always combined with a data coding process whereby extra bits are added to the serialized data stream in order to separate the individual digital words. Incidentally, in virtually all digital recording systems in use today the two stereo channels are multiplexed as well, with words from each channel following one another in an alternating sequence.

Multiplexing of two stereo channels of the same bandwidth cannot be done in the analog domain, which is why monophonic phonograph records recorded from a stereo master tape cannot be reproduced stereophonically, but it is easily accomplished in digital recording by the same parallel into the series process described a moment ago. The right and left channels are alternately input into a single bit stream with extra marking bits separating them, and then the original parallel output is reconstructed at output with no loss of information.

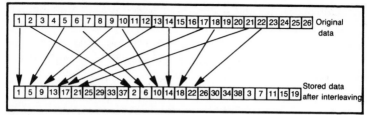

Fig. 4-6. Interfacing as used in CIRC.

CIRC

The next process used in digital recording is called *CIRC* error correction encoding, CIRC standing for the Cross Interleaved Reed Solomon Code.

The CIRC code has two purposes, preventing catastrophic losses of information, and enabling a decoder to detect any information losses should they occur. A CIRC decoder, which is part of the compact disc player, has provisions for reconstructing the lost signal—up to a point—should such losses be detected.

The CIRC encoder guards against losses by a process known as *interleaving.* Interleaving involves scrambling the bit stream and separating adjacent bits and distributing these bits many digits upstream. That way, if a tiny scratch appears on a compact disc obscuring several bits in a row, parts of several samples will be missing instead of one entire sample. It is easier to devise programs to fill in the blanks when sample information is incomplete in several samples rather than to recreate an entire sample based on the information in adjacent samples (Fig. 4-6).

The other aspects of CIRC, the introduction of *parity bits*, provides for a check on the integrity of the samples. Parity bits are additions to the signal that interrupt it at regular intervals and that take the form of a code of 1s and 0s that cannot be mistaken for the data comprising the audio signal itself. The flow of parity bits is monitored by a special circuit within the decoder, and if the flow is interrupted, the decoder knows that data has been destroyed.

The next stages in the digital recording process, namely subencoding, and channel modulation with 8 to 14-bit conversion, are peculiar to the compact disc, and are not present, at least in the same form, in other digital recording media. The purpose of these processes is to permit the 16-bit interleaved data stream to be incorporated in the specific physical medium of the compact disc. The two other physical media used for recording digitized audio signals, the rotary head video cassette recorder and the stationary head open real studio digital tape recorder, have their own distinct requirements that dictate other processes for manipulating the digital data.

The subencoding and the channel modulation are performed at the mastering stage just prior to the compact disc master being cut by the cutting laser. The digitized information on the reel-to-reel master tape has not been subjected to these manipulations, although it has been manipulated in other ways that won't concern us here. The subencoding and channel modulation are done instead as the digital data is being transferred from the reel-to-reel master to a 3/4 inch professional videocassette machine via a device known as a transcoder (video cassette machines are invariably used to transfer information to the cutting laser).

The subcode provides identification for the separate *frames* of digitized information. A frame is a division consisting of 6 samples from both channels. It is the smallest recognizable block of data and includes parity bits, synchronization bits required by the laser pickup mechanism, and a complete pattern of CIRC interleavings. The frame itself is further subdivided into 8 bit digital words.

The next process, channel modulation, involves converting the 8 bit words into a 14 bit code. This is done to ensure that a certain minimum distance will always be maintained between both pits and flats in the disc spiral so that information will not be misread. The encoding scheme also condenses the data so that each pit and flat can represent a string of 1s and 0s, and not just a single bit apiece, which subsequently increases the information storage capacity of the disc by an order of magnitude.

After 8 to 14 modulation has been completed, the information is ready to be transferred to the cutting laser that produces the compact disc master. At that point the digital encoding process is essentially complete.

DISC RECORDING

The basic digital encoding circuitry that has been described appears at the input of the master tape recorders used in the recording studio, not in the actual production facilities where compact discs are manufactured. As in the production of conventional phonograph records, the process of recording a master tape and cutting a disc are separate.

Compact discs go through a minimum of three generations or

transfers from one medium to another before they reach their final form. The first stage generally takes place in a recording studio where the actual performance is committed to magnetic tape (compact discs are never made directly from microphone feed though such a process is possible). As indicated earlier, a compact disc can be made from either a conventional analog reel-to-reel tape recording or from a digitally encoded reel-to-reel master tape. In either case, the information from the final two-track master must be transferred to a professional 3/4-inch video tape recorder prior to being fed into the CD cutting lathe, the actual machine that produces the disc master. For those unfamiliar with recording industry practice, following is an examination of the process step by step.

All but a handful of commercial recordings are made on multi track reel-to-reel tape recorders. In the case of classical recording, most of the machines in use today have digital encoders at input and accept the audio information onto the actual magnetic tape in digital form. In popular music, analog tape recorders are still the norm, although digital encoding is making rapid inroads.

This is not a book about the recording industry, but the reasons for the dominance of digital recording in the classical domain; its relative lack of penetration in the pop world bears examining.

We find two major reasons for the disparity. Most classical recordings are made by employees of the major record companies at recording facilities belonging to the major record companies. Those facilities happen to have digital tape recorders on hand because major record labels have collectively decided to support digital recording. Most popular recordings on the other hand are independently produced and are actually recorded at independent recording studios, most of which have simply not made the investment in digital tape recorders.

Why haven't they made the investment? Largely because of cost. Popular music producers record on 24 or 32 track machines, preferably 32 track tape recorders. Each track represents a separate channel of information and each can be adjusted in volume level relative to the other tracks. Thus, the producer can assign different instruments and voices or combinations of instruments and voices to individual tracks and juggle their levels relative to one another until the recording is set at the balance judged most pleasing. Eventually, the different tracks, for example 20, are mixed together into a smaller number of tracks, perhaps 12, and then, ultimately, into just two stereo tracks. The final result must be only two tracks, although the number of steps in the process and the number of tracks at each step may vary. It is possible to go directly via a device called a mixer from a 16 or 24 or 32 track master into a stereo cutting lathe, but it's almost never done due to the difficulty in balancing the tracks. The norm is to "mix down" in several stages, each of which is called a generation.

Unfortunately, 32 and 24 track digital tape recorders are extremely expensive—over $100,000 apiece—and most independent studios aren't willing to purchase them. (Classical recordings often involve no more than 16 tracks and less mixing down.) Pop producers get what they feel are adequate results on analog equipment, and they won't change until their equipment wears out and/or the price of 24 track digital recorders comes down (Fig. 4-7).

Whether the two track reel-to-reel master is analog or digital, it has to be transferred onto a two track 3/4" videotape prior to being sent to the compact disc manufacturing plant. Videotape is used rather than audio tape because it has room for the storage of a special operational code called a cue editor that enables the cutting lathe to translate the digital data into precisely timed bursts of laser light that, in turn, sear holes in the coated glass disc master.

From here on, the production of a compact disc rather closely resembles the production of a phonograph record. The cutting lathe

Fig. 4-7. Sony PCM 3324 24 track master tape recorder. This is the most widely used big multitrack digital system in the world, but at a price of over $100,000 it's too much for the smaller studios to afford. Courtesy of Sony Corporation.

71

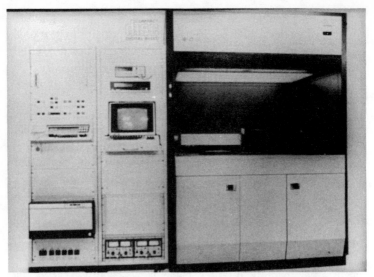

Fig. 4-8. A cutting laser in operation. Courtesy of Sony Corporation.

used to produce the disc master is a sort of reverse of a compact disc player with a similar focusing mechanism but with a vastly more powerful laser. The disc master, as indicated, is made of glass and is coated with a photoresistive substance. The laser cuts away portions of the photoresist, creating the pattern of pits and flats that will appear in the finished product (Figs. 4-8 and 4-9).

The pitted glass master is electroplated with a very thin layer of nickel to make a mold. This mold is called the matrix or father. The nickel plating is pulled off, a process that damages the master disc incidentally, and this thin plate is plated in turn and used to produce several metal mothers. The mothers, themselves, cannot be used to produce discs because they are positives of the disc itself and will produce pits where flats should be and vice versa. So the mother is also plated, and then used to produce stampers—the instruments that actually produce the compact disc (Fig. 4-10). The whole process of repeated platings is, essentially, similar to that used to make a phonograph record but it is far more exacting, because the spiral containing the digitized information is much smaller than is a record groove (Fig. 4-11).

In record production, stamping is the last significant phase of the manufacturing process. Beyond that only center hole punching and labeling remain. But the compact disc is a more complex object than a phonograph record, and stamping is followed by

72

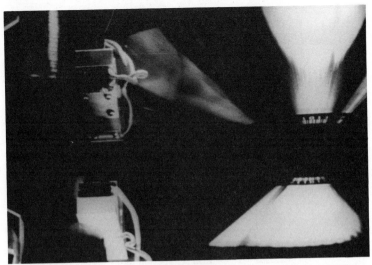

Fig. 4-9. Laser cutting machine for mastering compact discs. Courtesy of Sony Corporation.

several additional manufacturing steps.

The first of these is the center hole punching which is sometimes done in the stamper itself. The next step is the application of an extremely thin (100 nanometers) layer of reflective aluminum to the surface. The aluminum plating is vapor deposited and precisely fits the pitted contour of the disc. After the plating stage,

Fig. 4-10. Sony CDP 5000 compact disc mastering system used in quality control operations at pressing plants. Courtesy of Sony Corporation.

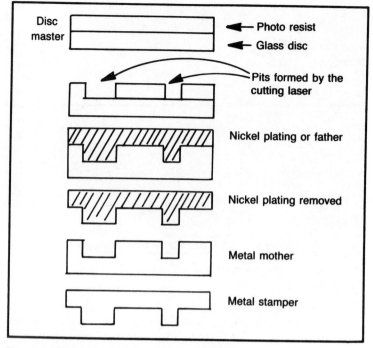

Fig. 4-11. Stages in the production of a compact disc.

the clear acrylic layer is applied with a spin coating machine and baked with ultraviolet light. Finally, the label is affixed to the acrylic, and the disc is ready for inspection and packaging.

DIGITAL DECODING AND DISC PLAYBACK

Demodulation. All digital tape recorders have both encoding and decoding circuitry. Compact disc players have only decoding circuitry. The decoding circuitry is essentially similar in both media, but the compact disc player is also equipped with a complex tracking mechanism for its laser eye which we have already described in Chapter 2.

In either tape or disc, once the encoded information contained in the recording medium has been converted into a series of electrical pulses, the decoding process proper can begin. In many but not all respects, it is the reverse of the encoding process (Fig. 4-12).

The first step is to extract the individual 1s and 0s that are relevant to the music signal from the succession of pits and flats on the disc. As mentioned earlier, the pits and flats themselves do not correspond precisely to the bit streams used to represent the original samples. Rather, they are a kind of cipher, a compressed, encoded form of that bit stream which also contains information relating to the beginning and ending of individual frames as well as parity bits for indicating information losses. The audio signal has to be separated from this background information in the first stage of decoding. In the compact disc format this first stage takes place in the *EFM* demodulator—EFM standing for eight to fourteen bit modulation.

But that's only the first stage of preliminary decoding. The next phase in the decode process sends the still digitized information to an *ERCO* (error correction) circuit where lost information is reconstructed by averaging the information in preceding samples. Prior to the actual error correction, the data stream is deinterleaved, that is, the bits are put back into their original sequence.

The ERCO circuits vary considerably from player to player with the better circuits averaging information over many preceding frames. Naturally, greater computing power is required as more frames are averaged, and greater computing power is reflected by greater costs. Thus, the most powerful error correction circuits tend to be found in the most expensive machines. The ERCO circuit (actually a series of circuits of diverse functions) also detects and corrects for speed errors at the rate that the information is read off the disc. The circuit contains a quartz oscillator producing a fixed frequency for comparison with the bit rate of the data stream. If the two do not coincide, a correction signal is sent to a servo control in the transport motor which makes appropriate adjustments in speed.

Following the ERCO circuit, things start to get complicated because the signal chain varies according to a number of different designs. Basically, three processes are involved—multiplexing, low pass filtering, and digital to analog conversion, but these processes do not always occur in the same order and, in the case of low pass filtering, three fundamentally different techniques are employed that result in considerable differences in the constitution of the sig-

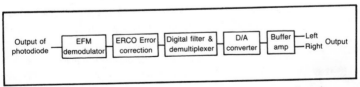

Fig. 4-12. Block diagram of decoding circuitry in a compact disc player.

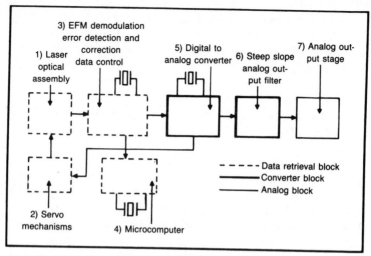

Fig. 4-13. Block diagram of conventional CD players. Courtesy of Sony Corporation.

nal chain from player to player (Fig. 4-13).

Output Filters. Most of the overall differences among machines do in fact arise from the type of filtering used at output. You will recall that steep antialiasing filters are used at input to prevent audio frequencies that are too high for the A/D convertor to sample from entering the system. Similar steep filters are used at output, but for a different reason.

Digital data takes the physical form of electrical pulses during transmission. Digital audio circuitry only responds to the coded information in the train of pulses. It does not register the actual waveforms of the individual pulses. When the time comes to translate the pulse train back into the original analog waveform of the audio input at the recording stage, the pulses are used to open a series of electronic gates that will release a continuous flow of electrical current, in other words, an analog waveform. Unfortunately this analog waveform will not be a perfect copy of the original but, instead, will be a ragged staircase shape that follows the approximate shape of the original, but that contains a multitude of sharp spikes. These spikes represent two types of spurious information. The first is the sampling frequency or clock which is a 44.1 kHz wave. The second is a series of complex high frequency bursts known as notch distortion caused by the nonlinearities of the gating transistors in the D/A convertor during turn on and turn off (Fig. 4-14).

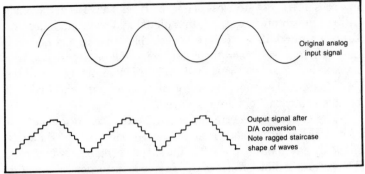

Fig. 4-14. Input and output signals.

If either the switching distortion or the clock frequency is allowed to enter the analog circuits of the audio system it will overload those circuits and will produce tremendous amounts of harsh, audible intermodulation distortion. Thus, both must be filtered out, especially the clock frequency.

Two basic methods of filtering are used. The first method, which is favored almost exclusively by Japanese manufacturers, is to use a single steep passive analog low pass filter. This, essentially, chops off high frequency energy from the signal and returns that energy to electrical ground. The low frequencies that contain the musical information are then passed on through the circuit. The second method also utilizes a low pass filter—actually two filters—but the first filter is not passive and involves considerable additional digital processing of the signal.

Passive Filters

For those unfamiliar with electronic filters, a passive filter, the first sort, is a circuit containing either capacitors or inductors or both, but never voltage amplifying transistors or vacuum tubes, the so-called active electronic circuit elements. Capacitors have the effect of offering increasing opposition to the flow of low frequency electrical impulses while inductors have the opposite effect, that is, they block high frequency impulses. The precise values of each determine the frequencies at which they begin to exert their effects. In simple low pass filters, only chokes are used, and in simple high pass filters capacitors are used exclusively.

However, a digital audio system in which filtering out high frequency impulses happens to be the primary consideration, the passive filters used to perform this function are far from simple. Simple low pass filters provide a loss of only 6 dB per octave as one ascends beyond the cutoff frequency. In a digital audio system a drop on the order of 60 dB per octave is desirable—that is, any high frequency impulses beyond the cutoff point will be suppressed to a level of 60 dB below the signal level within an octave above the 20 kHz limit. Therefore, very complex filters with multitudes of chokes and capacitors are employed.

The effect of these steep passive filters is to cause hundreds of degrees of phase shift near the cutoff point of 20 kHz and a marked "envelope distortion" in the shape of complex waveforms. The precise audible effects of this envelope distortion are a matter of considerable debate in the industry, with some authorities claiming the distortion is benign, others, that it is severely audible. Since filter components can have other detrimental effects on an audio signal such as harmonic distortion and time delays at certain frequencies that are not directly related to predicted phase shift, isolating the effects of envelope distortion in listening tests is difficult. Ideally, one would like to eliminate all phase shift and envelope distortion from an audio circuit, but failing that, some standards have to be developed as to what degree of and at what frequencies, envelope distortion is acceptable. Needless to say, universally accepted standards have not been formulated in this area (Fig. 4-15).

Digital Filters. The second type of filter, known as a digital filter, works much differently from the passive, though the end result is similar. Digital filtering, which involves complex active circuits with a multitude of transistors, albeit contained within tiny integrated circuits, can filter out high frequencies without producing appreciable degrees of phase shift. Such filters work by a process known as oversampling whereby the original samples are delayed and multiplied either two or four times so that each origi-

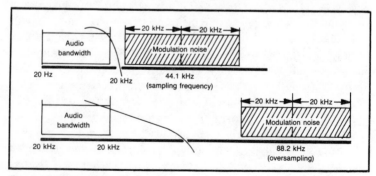

Fig. 4-15. Analog filter characteristics. Courtesy of Sony Corporation.

nal sample has a total of one or three duplicates. The oversampler itself has a clock frequency of either 88.2 or 176.4 kHz, two or four times the 44.1 kHz sampling rate.

What this oversampler does is move the problem up to a higher frequency range. The new clock has to be stripped away, and by a passive filter at that; but, because it is so high in frequency, a much less extreme filter can be used, one that will not cause as much phase shift. Before passive filtering, the oversampled system is decoded, so to speak, and the spurious high frequency content created by the original 44.1 kHz sampling process is removed by digital circuitry. In effect, the samples are averaged to produce a waveform of the same approximate configuration as in the original audio signal. The output of the D/A convertor is still a staircase shape, but it is close in appearance to an analog waveform with smaller spikes than is the case when oversampling is not used.

Digital filtering, it must be remembered, is always done before D/A conversion. Therefore, the D/A convertor must handle a digital data stream with two to four times the number of pulses and, thus, must be correspondingly faster. A second, passive filter is applied after D/A conversion just as in the purely passive filtering scheme. However in machines with digital filtering the passive filter is not especially steep.

Where a digital filter is used it will usually be combined with a demultiplexer; where the digital filter isn't present, the demultiplexer stands alone. The demultiplexer returns the serialized signal to parallel form prior to D/A conversion. It also separates the left channel from the right. However, in most compact disc players, true discrete stereo transmission only occurs after the D/A convertor because only one D/A convertor is used. During conversion, the output of one channel is delayed for about 11 microseconds while the other is converted to analog, then the delayed channel is converted while the other channel is delayed.

The next stage, digital-to-analog conversion is, in many respects, the most crucial part of the decoding process. Here, the digitized information, the pulses, activate electronic switches or gates that modulate continuous, analog current flows. The amplitude of the current at any particular instant will depend upon the number of 1s or on signals in the parallel digital messages. More 1s mean the gates release more current.

Several digital-to-analog convertors have been proposed or developed, the most rudimentary of which have a separate gate for each bit. Almost all current compact disc players use what is known as a dual slope integration or step integration digital-to-analog convertor. This device, which is similar to the dual slope integration analog-to-digital convertor in the encode circuitry, only has two gates controlling current flow, but has a pair of highly accurate counters between these gates and the parallel signals. The counters convert the parallel digital message into instructions for opening and closing the gates.

The output of the D/A convertor is an analog and not a digital signal, but it is not in the same form as the original analog audio signal at input. Thus it must be smoothed considerably before being passed on to the preamplifier.

Most compact disc players have sample and hold circuits (also called aperture circuits) following the digital-to-analog convertor that hold the outputs for tiny intervals of time before releasing them and will not accept new information from the convertor during those intervals. This is to allow voltages to stabilize within the convertor and reduce the magnitude of *switching glitches*, high frequency irregularities caused by the opening and closing of the electronic gates.

Following sample and hold, the signal is then run through a passive analog filter, a slow slope filter if oversampling and digital prefiltering have been used, a steep filter otherwise.

After filtering, the audio signal is fully analog and does not generally leave the analog realm during the rest of its journey through the audio system. Most compact disc players have analog amplifying circuits following the filters to match the electrical impedances of the signal to the next stage, which will generally be the auxiliary input of a preamplifier or receiver. From there on, the signal is handled no differently from the output of a tuner or a cassette deck.

Chapter 5

System Integration

The compact disc and the compact disc player represent radically new technologies within the field of consumer audio, but, as a consumer product, the compact disc player is intended to be easily integrated into existing component stereo systems. The purchase of a compact disc player does not absolutely require you to upgrade the rest of your system with "digital-ready" amplifiers and loudspeakers. Some compact discs—mostly classical releases—have sufficiently great dynamic range to place considerable stresses on a low wattage system, and if you own such a system and choose not to upgrade it, you will play such discs at your risk, but the majority of discs will place no more demands on your system than will phonograph records, simply because the dynamic range of the medium in most recordings is not exploited. A compact disc player will fit easily into most systems, though it will benefit from association with high quality amplifiers and speakers. The remainder of this chapter will be devoted to explaining how best an audio system may be set up around a compact disc player.

SETUP

A compact disc player is generally about the size of a stereo tuner and will weigh under 20 pounds. Power consumption will, generally, be under 50 watts, but the unit will tend to get moderately warm during operation. A free flow of air should be provided for the vents on the top and bottom of the machine, and these should never be obstructed. Most compact disc players are not readily rack-mountable.

So long as adequate ventilation is provided, the players can be placed almost anywhere—bookshelves, table, wooden equipment stands, etc. A level surface on a firm platform is preferable though, because the laser tracking mechanism is affected by vibration and will mistrack more frequently when vibrations are allowed to reach the disc-laser interface. It is immaterial whether such vibrations are caused by sound waves from the loudspeakers, footfalls, air conditioners, or whatever. Real fanatics may wish to invest in isolation stands—special mounting platforms that block vibrations ascending from the floor or from the piece of furniture where the player has been placed. Such isolation platforms take a number of forms. Dennesan, for instance, offers a 50 pound granite slab with optional pneumatic pods for support. This device probably affords the greatest degree of acoustic isolation of anything on the market, though, understandably, few persons wish to have such a slab on their bookshelves. A similarly imposing device is the Lead Balloon from Arcici, Inc., a metal stand heavily loaded with lead to damp out vibrations, and also weighing in the vicinity of 50 pounds (Fig. 5-1). More manageable isolation platforms are made by VPI and Torumat, the latter producing a small lightweight stand made from a honeycomb composite. All of these products come from small specialty companies and are poorly distributed. You are likely to find them only in audio salons catering to hobbyists, not in department stores or major electronic retail chains.

Wherever you put your compact disc player, you have to connect it to a stereo system to produce sound. It doesn't stand alone like a table radio. A compact disc player is ordinarily provided with a pair of RCA output jacks on the back panel. These jacks, which are marked "L" and "R" for left and right, accept terminations for a pair of left and right RCA interconnect cables. The cables are generally color-coded with the right termination colored red and the left, white or black. The opposite terminations are usually placed in the auxiliary input jacks of a preamplifier, receiver, or integrated amplifier (Fig. 5-2).

Here some definitions are in order: between a *signal source* such as a compact disc player, radio, tape deck, or phonograph, and a pair of loudspeakers which actually move the air in your listening room and produce sound, lay several stages of electronic amplification. That is because a loudspeaker is, essentially, a kind of electric motor and it requires a high power input signal to generate

Fig. 5-1. Lead Balloon Isolation Stand pictured with a JVC QL-75 turntable. The Lead Balloon can be just as easily used with compact disc players. The Lead Balloon uses lead bars atop a steel platform to isolate components from vibrations. It is quite effective. Courtesy of Arcici Incorporated.

audible sound. The feeble electrical signals produced by sound sources are simply insufficient to power a full-sized domestic loudspeaker and, thus, the signals must be boosted in an amplifier.

An audio amplifier may be likened to a series of electronic valves, or gates; the input signal triggers a "valve" producing a flow of electricity that shares the wave form of the signal but is

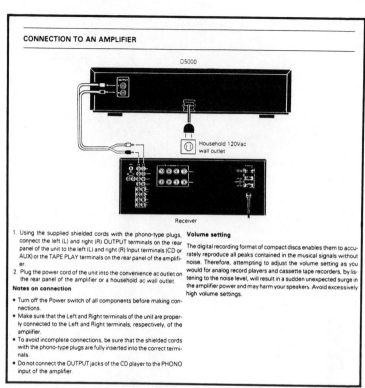

D5000

Household 120Vac
wall outlet

Receiver

1. Using the supplied shielded cords with the phono-type plugs,
connect the left (L) and right (R) OUTPUT terminals on the rear
panel of the unit to the left (L) and right (R) Input terminals (CD or
AUX) or the TAPE PLAY terminals on the rear panel of the amplifier.

2. Plug the power cord of the unit into the convenience ac outlet on
the rear panel of the amplifier or a household ac wall outlet.

Notes on connection

• Turn off the Power switch of all components before making connections.

• Make sure that the Left and Right terminals of the unit are properly connected to the Left and Right terminals, respectively, of the
amplifier.

• To avoid incomplete connections, be sure that the shielded cords
with the phono-type plugs are fully inserted into the correct terminals.

• Do not connect the OUTPUT jacks of the CD player to the PHONO
input of the amplifier.

Volume setting

The digital recording format of compact discs enables them to accurately reproduce all peaks contained in the musical signals without
noise. Therefore, attempting to adjust the volume setting as you
would for analog record players and cassette tape recorders, by listening to the noise level, will result in a sudden unexpected surge in
the amplifier power and may harm your speakers. Avoid excessively
high volume settings.

Fig. 5-2. Back panel of a Shure D5000 Compact Disc Player showing hookup
to a receiver. Courtesy of Shure Brothers.

greater in amplitude, and that output then serves as the input to
the next stage and so on until a flow of electricity millions of times
greater than the input signal is eventually produced. In modern tran-
sistorized audio systems a half dozen or so stages of amplification
may occur between the sound source and the loudspeaker, and
usually all but the last stage will produce mainly voltage gain, not
current gain. The final stage, on the other hand, will produce a slight
voltage drop, but a massive current gain and a consequent power
gain as well.

Traditionally, at least since the 1950s, the voltage amplification stages have been divided up between two separate components,
the preamplifier and the amplifier. The *preamplifier* also contains
a volume control, circuitry for contouring the signal from a phono
cartridge, mechanical switches for choosing between sound sources,
and, in some cases, tone controls. Most of the circuitry in a preamp
is, in fact, concerned with the signal from the phono cartridge and

if, as many predict, the phonograph passes into obsolescence sometime in the 1990s, we may expect that the preamplifier will gradually disappear as well.

The *amplifier*, or power amplifier as it's known, traditionally has no volume or tone controls and few or no features. It is basically just a metal box full of amplifying circuitry and, perhaps equipped with meters or LED displays on the front panel. Its inputs are generally RCA jacks, but the outputs are apt to vary from model to model. Banana jacks or binding posts are the most common output connectors. Binding posts are preferable (Fig. 5-3).

Power amplifiers and preamplifiers may be combined in a single component called an *integrated amplifier*. If a radio is added, one has a receiver. In the United States, the majority of component stereo systems utilize receivers rather than a separate power amp and preamp or an integrated amplifier (Fig. 5-4).

Whatever the setup—separates, integrated amplifier, or receiver—a compact disc player's output is ordinarily routed into the *line amplifier* stage of the preamplifier (remember, receivers and

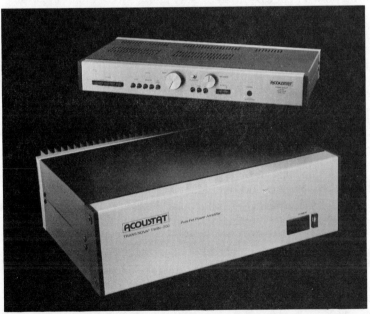

Fig. 5-3. Acoustat Transnova preamplifier and amplifier. Both use field effect transistors exclusively and very innovative circuit topologies. Acoustat Corporation has made electronics for many years, but is better known for electrostatic loudspeakers. Note relate sizes of amp and preamp. Courtesy of Acoustat Corporation.

Fig. 5-4. Yamaha A-1020 integrated amplifier. Integrated amplifiers combine a preamplifier and power amplifier in one chassis. Courtesy of Yamaha Electronics.

integrated amplifiers contain preamplifier sections). A compact disc player's output can be fed directly into the RCA inputs of a power amplifier, thus bypassing the line amplifier of the preamp, but unless the power amp has a volume control, which few do, or unless the compact disc player itself has a volume control, you have no way of controlling the volume level of the music. The advantage of such direct input to the power amp is that the minor distortions of the line amp are avoided, however, the electrical impedance match between compact disc player and amplifier may not be optimal. You might try experimenting with both types of hookup if you're inclined—that is if your amp has volume controls.

The actual RCA cables you use to connect the player with the next component in the signal chain have become subject to considerable product differentiation of late and vary in price from under a dollar a meter-pair up to nearly $200.00 retail for the same length! The mass distribution audio magazines have generally pooh-poohed the idea that there are any audible differences between cables, but at least some blind listening tests have tended to support the notion that choice of cable can make an audible difference in the sound of a system. Whether one wants to spend $200 for admittedly subtle improvements is another matter. I, personally, use cables made of the new large crystal copper wiring manufactured by Hitachi, and I find them to be worth their considerable cost. However, little consensus exists among audio reviewers on the matter of cables, some favoring the sound of one, others that of another. I find the pricing of exotic cables to be exorbitant to say the least. Unless you are spending a great deal of money on the rest of the system and selecting really premium components, spending a couple of hundred dollars on wiring for your system is ill-advised, although in the case of loudspeakers use of thin gauge "lamp cord" will noticeably degrade the sound. But more on this later.

Whatever wiring you choose to use, it's always a good idea to make sure that cable terminations are free from grease, corrosion, or other foreign elements that increase electrical resistance. Heavily gold-plated, corrosion-resistant terminations are advisable and are provided on most of the high-priced exotic cables. Some compact disc players have gold-plated RCA jacks as well—a desirable feature. Application of electrical contact cleaners such as Blue Shower or Cramolin to terminations prior to hookup is always a good idea even if such terminations are gold-plated.

Other than cleaning contacts, providing ventilation, and selecting a stable, level surface, set up of a compact disc player presents few problems. Ideally, it's good to have a separate circuit for your audio system, because refrigerators and other power-hungry appliances can disturb the operation of CD players and other audio components, but, certainly, a separate circuit is not a necessity. Compact disc players are designed to handle some fluctuation in line voltage levels, and they are also designed to be fairly immune to *ground loops*—situations occurring when 60 cycle hum and interference from other components are manifested in the signal because of poor grounding. Compact disc players themselves do, in use, transmit a certain amount of low level radio frequency interference (r.f.) from the operation of their digital circuitry, but the level of the interference is seldom high enough to have audible effects on other components.

"DIGITAL READINESS" AND DESIRABLE COMPONENT ATTRIBUTES

Even before the compact disc format was released in this country, manufacturers of amplifiers, receivers, loudspeakers, and even cassette recorders were making free use of the phrase "digital ready" in describing their equipment—suggesting that older components might not be quite up to the task of reproducing digitally encoded music. The industry as a whole saw the compact disc as a promotional opportunity for selling complete new audio systems and, indeed, sales of all audio components except turntables and cartridges have increased in the last two years, probably as a result of CD-induced upgrades. But in spite of manufacturers' assurances of the digital readiness of their products, the design of preamps, amps, receivers and loudspeakers has changed hardly at all as a result of the introduction of the compact disc.

On the average, receivers and mass produced integrated amplifiers have a little more power than before, but even there the increase is so modest as to be fairly inconsequential. In buying a current model of audio component one has no assurance that it's any better suited to the exigencies of digital reproduction than the models of five years ago. Buying new equipment in the belief that it's somehow better matched to the compact disc medium is then clearly misguided.

But the consumer is still left with the question of what demands the compact disc player really makes on other components and what component choices will result in the best sound quality and in the greatest operational reliability of the system. The rest of this chapter focuses on these concerns.

The following is a consideration of each of the components in the order in which they appear in the signal patch.

The Preamplifier

A separate preamplifier is generally only going to be present in an expensive "high end" audio system. Nevertheless, all component stereo systems contain preamplifiers—generally included within the receiver, so the following remarks can be easily applied to the preamp section of a receiver, or an integrated amplifier for that matter.

A preamplifier contains essentially two blocks of circuitry, a phono amp and a line amp. The *phono amp* handles the output from a phono cartridge and won't concern us here. A *line amp* accepts the output of all other sound sources, tuner, cassette deck, VCR, laser disc player, and compact disc player.

The line amp has two major functions in an audio system. First, it provides a certain amount of amplification to the signal coming from the sound source, but more important, it matches the electrical impedance of the signal output to the input requirements of the power amplifier.

Preamps ordinarily only have one line amplifier section, but they usually have several line inputs and these multiple line inputs are a matter of some confusion. Up until a couple of years ago, the typical preamp had three line-level inputs—generally designated "tape," "tuner," and "aux" (auxiliary). All of these inputs were,

Fig. 5-5. Nova CPA-100, a "purist" preamplifier with no tone controls. The Nova has generous overload capabilities and is unlikely ever to be stressed by a CD input. Courtesy of Nova Acoustics.

in fact, identical. The designations were simply given to aid the user in hooking up the system. A series of mechanical switches on the front panel also marked tape, tuner, and aux enabled the user to feed any one of these inputs into the single line amp—but only one of them at a time (Fig. 5-5). With the appearance of new formats such as the laser disc, VCR, and compact disc, the traditional three-line inputs became inadequate and now preamps may come equipped with five or more line inputs, one of which is usually labelled "CD" (Fig. 5-6). In all but a couple of cases which will be considered in a later chapter, the CD input is no different from the other line inputs.

Traditionally, preamp design has focused on the phono amp section where amplification and equalization problems are extremely critical and the line amp has tended to be overlooked, lacking in design elegance, and sometimes even lacking in adequate

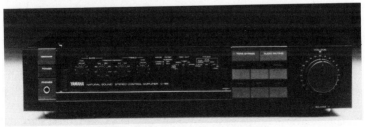

Fig. 5-6. Yamaha C-65 preamplifier. A fully featured unit at a much lower price than the Nova, the C-65 includes a two band parametric equalizer. Courtesy of Yamaha Electronics.

performance specifications. As a result, many preamps have line amp sections that are really not up to reproducing the full dynamic range of the CD medium. The preamp sections of integrated amplifiers and receivers are apt to be especially bad in this regard. A key specification, one not usually supplied by the manufacturer, is overload capability. A compact disc player produces a maximum output of 2.5 volts. If the line amplifier has an overload capability of less than this it simply cannot handle the maximum output and will "clip" the top off of waves of that magnitude and will consequently feed a distorted signal into the power amplifier. Surprisingly, old fashioned vacuum tube preamps generally perform very well in this regard. To be on the safe side, an overload capability of 5 volts rather than 2.5 is desirable in a preamp and such a specification is fairly common in high quality units.

Additional design characteristics that make for unstressed reproduction of dynamic musical signals are large, preferably separate, power supplies and dual monaural construction.

The *power supply* is the reservoir of electrical energy from which the preamp draws to replicate the input signal. A large supply does not, itself, ensure flawless reproduction, but all perfectionist cost-is-no-object preamps boast large supplies, and increasing numbers of moderately priced units have them as well.

What's large? A preamp with a generous supply will weigh at least 10 pounds—perhaps more than 20. The filter capacitors within the supply, that are used to smooth the direct current supplied to the signal circuitry, will have a collective rating in the thousands of microfarads at the very least.

A separate power supply is one that has its own metal housing (such supplies are connected to the main chassis of the preamp by a short length of heavy cable, generally supplied by the manufacturer). This mode of construction serves to shield the signal circuitry from transformer hum and generally results in less noise being transmitted through the system. It also greatly increases the cost of the unit since the sheet metal housings are normally the most expensive single part of any electronic component (Fig. 5-7).

Dual monaural construction, again generally found only in fairly expensive equipment, is the provision of a separate power supply for each channel. This reduces crosstalk—leakage of information between channels—and results in clearer sound. It also ensures that a particularly loud passage favoring one channel will not cause blurred reproduction in the other channel as sometimes happens with conventional stereo preamps.

Fig. 5-7. Krell PAM-3. The Krell has a separate power supply housed in its own chassis and a special CD input with selectable phase compensation and post emphasis for various models of CD player. Courtesy of Krell Industries.

Amplifiers

The preamp is followed by the power amplifier in most systems. (In bi and tri-amplified systems which we will consider later in this chapter, the preamp is followed by an electronic crossover and then by two or more amplifiers.) Between these two components a pair of RCA interconnect cables is generally run, identical in kind to those connecting the CD player to the preamp.

Amplifiers, regardless of statements to the contrary that sometimes appear in the popular audio press, make a major difference in the sound of an audio system. In terms of the ubiquitous total harmonic distortion specification they may all look pretty good, but model to model performance varies considerably.

An amplifier is best considered in the light of the type of musical signals it will be called upon to reproduce and, even more important, the type of loudspeakers it will be required to drive. Some amplifiers work well in all applications, but they generally cost a lot and there's no sense paying for something unless you need it. So how do you determine what you actually do need?

The most readily apparent differences among amplifiers are their power and current ratings. By law all domestic amplifiers sold in the United States must produce their stated power into an 8 ohm electrical load according to the strict r.m.s rating standard. Manufacturers rarely fudge in meeting this requirement, and most amps will make rated power and then some. This power rating gives you at least some basis for choice.

Power requirements for your system can be determined by establishing the sound pressure levels at which you wish to listen and then ascertaining the efficiency rating of your loudspeakers. The less efficient the speakers are the more power you will need per a given sound pressure level. Speakers are generally rated for efficiency by stating the sound pressure level produced directly in front of the speaker at a distance of one meter with an input of one watt of power. Typical stated efficiency ratings range from about 80 dB at one watt at one meter to 95 dB at one watt at one meter.

However, here I have found that speaker manufacturers do often fudge—sometimes by as much as 10 dB. Sometimes the only way to get an idea of a speaker's efficiency is to audition it and see how far you have to twist the volume control to get a satisfactory sound level. I've seen differences in dial position of over 180 degrees between speakers.

The speaker's output at one watt gives you a base for calculating the amplifier power you will need. If your speakers are rated at 85 dB efficiency and you never listen to any music with peaks exceeding 90 dB, you'd only need an amplifier of five watts (remember, every 3 dB increase in sound pressure level requires a doubling of amplifier power). Remember too, however, that there is often a big difference between average listening level and the peak level of a recording. Particularly in classical music, peak levels may be 30 or 40 dB louder than average levels and the compact disc medium was designated to capture these contrasts. If you listen to classical music at an average level of 80 dB on compact disc you may get musical peaks of 110 dB or more.

Now let's go back to our 85 dB speaker and see what that means. Using our doubling for every 3 dB formula, we find that over 300 watts are required to reach those 110 dB peaks.

Then what happens if you use an amplifier of less than the required power? That depends on the design of the amp. An amplifier's output is a function of input voltage up to the overload point—which is not always the same as the related maximum power. Beyond that point, the amplifier will do one of two things. It will either supply extra power on a short-term basis, or it will go straight into clipping, that is, it will produce increasing amounts of distortion as the input voltage exceeds the overload point.

An amplifier that behaves in the first manner is said to have *dynamic headroom*. Such headroom is frequently stated in standard specifications and is measured in terms of dB, dB being related to power by the familiar formula. Thus, an amplifier with 3 dB headroom will double power on a short term basis.

Dynamic headroom sounds like a very desirable attribute in an amplifier but, unfortunately, the usual way of achieving it is through an under-engineered power supply. A power supply is supposed to hold the voltages of the electrical current it supplies to the power transistors at some fixed value with minimal variation (power supply voltages are commonly referred to as voltage rails or supply rails). The rail voltages determine the power the amplifier can put out, and the higher the voltage the more power. If the rails are absolutely fixed, obviously, so is the maximum power level.

In amplifiers with headroom, the supply rails "sag," that is, the voltages go way down on a momentary basis and the power supply is momentarily drained. The output transistors are no longer held under constant operating conditions and their performance becomes nonlinear. Such nonlinearity is not apt to show up on a static distortion test at rated power, but subjective reviewers frequently complain about lack of bass impact and confused imaging and loss of detail at high volume levels in amplifiers with high headroom.

Another problem with high headroom designs is that the headroom is very momentary and peak power is provided for only a tiny fraction of a second. Strong bass impulses such as synthesizer blasts or pipe organ pedal points can easily exceed headroom *duration* and at that point the amp goes into hard clipping.

A more sophisticated way of obtaining headroom is through class G operation or "stacked supplies." Here, instead of loading down a single underengineered supply, the amplifier utilizes a pair of power supplies. Except at very high power levels, the amplifier works off only one supply; the second supply is switched into the circuit to provide brief spurts of additional power.

Class G operation is a sounder method of providing headroom than loading down and single small supply because it permits at least one supply to maintain constant supply voltages, but such class G amplifiers may suffer from switching noise as the second supply enters the circuit and, in addition, the incorporation of two supplies necessarily increases cost of manufacturing. Class G amps still suffer from the traditional problem of all high headroom designs—they can't provide extra power for more than a very brief time span (Fig. 5-8). In sum, high continuous power capabilities

Fig. 5-8. Soundcraftsman DDR 1200. Another extremely high power amplifier, one relying on stacked supplies, and technically classified as a class G type power amplifier, though Soundcraftsman prefers the term class H, justifying the nomenclature by some unusual circuit topology.

are always better than dynamic headroom.

Apart from headroom, another consideration in accessing an amplifier's performance at the limits of power is its behavior while clipping. Most amplifiers clip hard, that is, they produce a burst of odd order high frequency distortion that sounds harsh and offensive and that can overload and burn out tweeters, the high frequency elements on a conventional loudspeaker. Old fashioned vacuum tube amplifiers (which, incidentally, are still manufactured by Audio Research, Conrad Johnson, and a few other companies) do not have this characteristic when clipping. They stay sweet sounding and merely get soft and fuzzy—producing mostly second and third order harmonic distortion. A few—a very few—solid state amps have this same characteristic. It tends to be associated with class A operation in which the amp is biased very hard and conducts large amounts of current at all times. Unfortunately, class A amps are expensive both to buy and to operate, and are usually fairly low-powered to boot (Fig. 5-9).

Sheer power is far from the only consideration when selecting an amplifier. Current capability is also extremely important and has a direct bearing on the power the amp will deliver into speaker loads which depart from the standard 8 ohm resistive impedance.

Loudspeaker inputs offer certain values of electrical resistance to the amplifier that drives them—generally fairly low values. In accordance with Ohm's law (see Glossary) resistance determines the power that the amplifier will actually deliver into the loudspeaker load. If the amplifier has to overcome a large electrical resistance, it will deliver less power, and the reduction in power will be linear—that is, a doubling of resistance will result in a halving of power. Most loudspeakers on the market have a nominal or stated impedance of 8 ohms and, thus, amplifiers are typically rated according to the power they can deliver into 8 ohms. It follows that most amps, deliver only half their rated power into 16 ohm loudspeaker impedances (nominal 16 ohm speakers, though once common, have, thankfully, almost vanished from the market).

Amps with well engineered power supplies deliver correspondingly more power into loads that are lower than 8 ohms, and here again the relation should be linear though it isn't necessarily. That is, ideally, an amplifier delivering 100 watts into 8 ohms should deliver 200 into 4 ohms and 400 into 2 ohms. In fact, very few amplifiers can quadruple power into 2 ohms and most won't even double power into 4 ohms.

To deliver more power into low impedance loads, an amplifier must have a high current capacity. Power, that is, wattage, equals current times voltage, and since most modern amplifiers deliver constant voltages at output, the only way they can increase power is to increase current flow. But why should an amp be able to deliver more power into low impedance loads in the first place? What's the purpose if most loudspeakers are actually 8 ohms?

Well, it turns out that most loudspeakers aren't actually 8 ohms, at least not over their entire frequency range. Most loudspeakers may, indeed, have a model impedance of roughly 8 ohms, but at the same time they may have impedance peaks of over 20 ohms

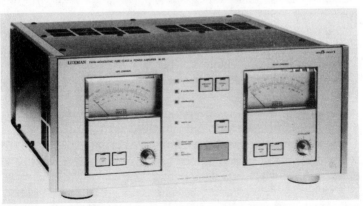

Fig. 5-9. Luxman M-05 pure class A power amp—one of the few in existence. Class A amps have tube-like distortion spectra and generally clip softly. This one at 105 watts per channel is moderately high powered.

and impedance dips of down to less than an ohm. Worse yet, the impedance may become *reactive* at certain frequencies, that is, the loudspeaker load may exhibit capacitative and inductive components. Inductance and capacitance in the speaker load increase the current demands on the amplifier still further.

Amplifiers with poor current capability characteristically have difficulty driving highly reactive speaker loads such as presented by electrostatic loudspeakers, and even with conventional loudspeakers, low current amplifiers tend to exhibit dips in frequency response at precisely those frequencies that the impedance varies markedly from the nominal 8 ohms.

Manufacturers sometimes list current capability in specifications, but they seldom differentiate between instantaneous current capability which is a variant of dynamic headroom and continuous current capability which is what really counts. Anything over 15 amperes of continuous current capability is commendably high.

If current capability is not supplied in the manufacturer's specifications, a clue is provided by the size of the amplifier. High continuous current capability requires a physically bulky power supply. High current amplifiers of even modest power ratings tend to be heavy, weighing at least 30 pounds and often much more. Receivers virtually never have high current amplifier sections due to weight considerations, and high current amplifiers sections are rare in integrated amplifiers.

The lack of current capability becomes particularly rankling when the loudspeakers in the system have four rather than eight-ohm nominal impedance ratings, as an increasing number of loudspeakers do. An amplifier that is not rated to deliver a continuous output into four ohms will sound oddly compressed and lacking in dynamics. You see, most amplifiers have a protective circuit called a current limiter which limits current flow from the power supply when the output impedance dips below a certain point. That's because output power transistors will burn up if forced to pass excessive current. In some amplifiers, mainly those found in receivers, the current limiter comes into play at impedances of over four ohms and a four ohm continuous load will trigger the limiter more or less continuously. A system driven by such an amplifier will still play music, but the music will lack impact.

High current has recently become a buzz word in audio advertising, and numerous manufacturers claim to produce high current amplifiers and receivers. There really has been a broad gauge improvement in amplifiers in regard to current capability in recent years, but plenty of units on the market, particularly Japanese receivers and integrated amplifiers, still provide very limited current.

The above remarks relating to amplifier power and current are relevant to any domestic audio system and not just one built around a compact disc player. The power and current issues seem a little more pressing in regard to the new medium only because the dynamic range of the compact disc has greater potential for pushing amps to their limits.

Power and current capability are the paramount performance parameters for power amps, but there are others to consider. Most amplifiers specify a *damping factor* the ratio of the amplifier's own output impedance to the 8 ohm loudspeaker impedance. An amplifier's output impedance is generally far less than 8 ohms, and specified damping factors may be as high as 500 to 1 for some frequencies, a figure that represents an effective output impedance for the amplifier of a little over a hundredth of an ohm.

The damping factor is a confusing and much debated specification. It is supposed to represent the amplifier's ability to control the loudspeaker by bringing the loudspeaker drivers or sound producing elements to an abrupt stop after the music signal has passed through its circuits. The amplifier itself represents something close to a short circuit to the electrical energy being generated by the magnet structures of the drivers, and this short circuit functions as an electrical brake on cone motion. The lower the output impedance of the amp the closer the output circuits come to being a short circuit and the greater the braking effect.

All things being equal, the higher the damping factor the better, at least in theory, but in damping factors, as in many other aspects of amplifier performance, there is a law of diminishing returns, and the utility of damping factors beyond about 50 to 1 has not been conclusively demonstrated.

The damping factor specification tends to be misleading in other ways as well. High damping factors are commonly thought to be more important in the low frequency range and are often specified only at low frequencies so the consumer gets little idea of damping performance in the midrange and treble. Thus, an amplifier with a damping factor of 100 at 50 Hz might have a factor of less than 10 at 10 kHz, although some types of loudspeakers benefit from high damping factors for the treble frequencies. Then too, the crossover network of the loudspeaker and the audio cables used to transmit power from the amplifier both have fairly high resistive values and effectively reduce the damping factor the amplifier actually presents to the loudspeaker driver. Because of these conditions, probably no amplifier has an effective damping factor higher than about 20 to 1 unless it is used as part of a bi or triamplified system, and the loudspeaker's passive crossover network is bypassed.

In those cases that the output impedance of the amplifier is low, say a tenth of an ohm, it will become almost negligable in the actual damping factor pertaining to the loudspeaker driver, the resistance of the wire and crossover will dominate the load seen by the driver. Further reduction of amplifier output impedance will make little change in the equation and may actually result in a worse sounding amplifier if such reduction is achieved by huge values of global negative feedback, as is usually the case. (More will be said on feedback in the following subsection.)

Some other amplifier specifications of some importance, though rarely given in standard specs, relate to bandwidth. Solid state amplifiers (tube amps are a special case) usually have the ability to reproduce signals that are considerably higher in frequency than audible sound waves. Manufacturers of high quality power amplifiers not only strive for high frequency extensions but for full power delivery at least up to 50 kHz and low distortion specifications for the ultrasonic region as well. The reason for this seemingly extravagant high frequency performance is to prevent the amplifier from overloading and going into clipping when confronted with spurious ultrasonic signals or from generating distortion in the presence of an ultrasonic musical signal. The importance of avoiding clipping is obvious. Clipping tends to be very audible. But the rationale behind reducing ultrasonic distortion is less apparent.

Ultrasonic signals, whether representing spurious "garbage" created by poorly functioning audio circuits or the very high frequency musical overtones captured in some analog recordings, are present to a surprising degree in the signals passing into the amplifier from the line amp. If the amp has poor ultrasonic performance it will create large amounts of distortion above the audible region. These distortions, which are higher in frequency than the ultrasonic signal itself, will not be heard directly but may intermodulate with the audio signal and create IM distortions in the audible range. In extreme cases, an amp with poor high frequency performance will create high order distortion products of very great magnitude in the presence of signals within the audio range, and although these distortion products will be above 20 kHz, they will intermodulate with the music signal and create a lot of irritating

IM. It might be added that tests conducted in the popular audio magazines frequently do not include any distortion readings above 20 kHz. The poorly designed amplifier will be producing very high values of ultrasonic distortion and probably a good measure of IM in the audible bandwidth, and yet the specs will proclaim THD at 0.05%!

Of course, these same publications and most manufacturers rarely provide specifications relating to IM distortion, either. This common omission may be attributed to the fact that IM distortion is the Achilles Heel of many amplifiers.

The other significant performance parameter relating to bandwidth is slew rate, which represents the rate at which the amplifier's circuits can respond to changes in signal voltages. The time interval for representing slew rate is one microsecond—one millionth of a second. The change is represented in volts, so the full measurement is volts per microsecond.

Music signals themselves contain impulses that constitute changes in energy level on the order of about six volts in one microsecond at the maximum. Early solid state amps with slew rates of under 5 volts per microsecond were clearly inadequate to handle such signals, but most everything on the market today has a slew rate of at least 10 volts per microsecond. Many electronics engineers feel that a considerable safety margin is advisable and advocate slew rates of at least 20 and preferable 50 volts or better. Since amplifiers with such slew rates are readily available and at moderate prices, you might as well purchase a high slew rate unit if you're building a quality, audio system.

As I indicated in Chapter 3, I do not believe that extremely low total harmonic distortion specifications are, in themselves, very desirable. Indeed, a good case might be made for buying an amplifier with relatively high harmonic distortion, say 0.1 percent instead of the usual 0.005 percent. That is because low distortion is generally obtained not by careful circuit design and use of low distortion transistors, but by the dubious practice of using very high values of global negative feedback. Negative feedback is the routing of part of the output signal of a transistor amplifier back around to its input and reverses its phase in the process. Negative feedback cancels out part of the signal and has the effect of reducing both the distortion of the circuit and the amplification factor of the transistor. You get less distortion but you also get less boost. The reduction in amplification is less a problem than it seems since you can always add another gain stage. Without going into the mathematics of the process, it can be stated that by using plenty of feedback and multiple gain stages one can get all the power he wants and harmonic distortion figures so low that they're scarcely measurable.

Feedback sounds great, and it certainly has its uses, but the employment of large values of global feedback—that is, a feedback loop around the entire amplifying circuit—has become associated with a kind of shrill, metallic tonal characteristic in sound reproduction. High feedback amps tend to perform well on standard tests but they also tend to fall down in the reproduction of ultrasonics and in IM tests because the feedback loops become progressively inoperative as frequency rises, and because while feedback tends to produce less distortion overall it increases the proportion of high order distortions within the total distortion product. Feedback also exacerbates TIM, or voltage clipping, by artificially extending the high frequency response of transistors to regions where they do not perform linearly.

Large values of global feedback (above about 35 dB) have been very largely abandoned in the more costly solid state power amplifiers, but they are typical of lower priced equipment, particularly receivers. But in spite of the disrepute in which high feedback is held and its absence in "flagship" models, it will probably continue to be used in mass produced components for two reasons. First, it's inexpensive. The designer can take a basically low spec circuit made of low grade, poorly matched parts and clean it up with feedback. Second, it produces impressive specs that are difficult to obtain by other means. It may be possible to get 0.005 percent THD with 12 dB of global feedback, but it can't be done easily or cheaply.

This discussion of power amplifiers is concluded with the observation that amplifier manufacturers devote a great deal of energy to touting various circuit refinements and innovations, including "new class A operation," "real phase power supplies," "magnetic field operation," MOSFET output transistors, and so on. Such high-lighting of isolated circuit refinements totally obscures the fact that many proven designs exist today for producing good sounding amplifiers and that the success or failure of any amplifier will be heavily dependent on parts quality, care of manufacture, particularly circuit calibration and testing, and perhaps most of all on the engineering of the power supply. Most amplifiers built today use essentially similar circuit topologies in the signal path. The execution of the circuit, the power ratings of the transistors, and the provision of adequate heat dissipation are the main variables in performance, not basic design. Isolated circuit refinements will no more make a poor performer into a standout than adding extra cylinder valves will make a generally undetuned automobile engine into a racing mill.

In any case, the most important factor to consider in choosing any amplifier is not test bench performance but how well it interfaces with the particular loudspeaker system that it is intended to drive. The choice of loudspeakers should dictate the choice of the amplifier. It should never be bought as an isolated purchase.

Loudspeakers

The loudspeaker is the final link in the signal chain and the only part of an audio system that actually produces sound. Like a microphone or a phono cartridge, it is a transducer, that is, it transforms one kind of energy (electrical) into another, (mechanical) and then that energy to still another (acoustical).

Loudspeakers, as a component category, exhibit the greatest degree of variation, both in design and in performance. Changing loudspeakers is apt to result in more obvious and readily identifiable differences in the sound quality of an audio system than changes made elsewhere in the signal chain. For this reason, many popular publications on home audio have urged the consumer to concentrate on loudspeakers, and some popular writers have even asserted that a good pair of loudspeakers will yield excellent performance with practically any signal source and amplifier. Often in these same popular publications, the reader is enjoined to spend half the total amount of money allocated for an audio system on the loudspeakers.

My own view is otherwise. Loudspeakers are certainly of paramount importance in the ultimate performance of any audio system, but they are far from the only factor in system performance. The popular audio press stresses speaker performance over that of other components because of editorial policies built around noncritical product reviews. Differences among other component categories other than loudspeakers are subtler and harder to categorize, and thus can be said not to exist. Since differences among loudspeakers are too obvious to be denied, the popular press inevitably focuses on the loudspeaker, though even within that category it tends to report only the most obvious differences relating to dispersion and frequency response.

So what really is important in loudspeaker performance and in what areas of performance must one look for the most significant differences among loudspeakers? To answer these questions, I will attempt to define some basic performance parameters, especially as they relate to compact disc reproduction.

First, frequency response: Loudspeakers are the only audio components that generally do not have usable frequency response over the full audible range, and that commonly exhibit gross variations in frequency response. Most loudspeakers on the market are especially deficient in deep bass performance, and there the deficiency tends to be closely related to size and price. Very few low priced loudspeakers will play full volume as low as 30 Hz. Very few loudspeakers at any price will play at full volume down to 20 Hz, the lower limit of the compact disc. In contrast, all but a handful of amplifiers will pass 20 Hz tones with ease. In other words, if your speakers can play to 20 Hz, most amps will drive them.

The ability of a loudspeaker to play deep bass is closely related to two factors, the size of the speaker enclosure and the size of the woofer, the low frequency sound producing element. These, in turn, relate to price simply because big woofers and big enclosures cost more to manufacture. Woofers with diameters of less than 10 inch rarely produce deep bass, that is, base in the 30 Hz range, and a speaker with less than a 15 inch woofer is unlikely to have response down to 20 Hz. To be sure, many speakers with 15 inch woofers have a much higher bass cutoff point because the system is deliberately tuned to a higher frequency for reasons of efficiency, but accomplishing the opposite, that is, tuning a system with a small woofer to a lower frequency cutoff, is extremely difficult and seldom produces really satisfactory results (Fig. 5-10).

It's harder to generalize about enclosure size and bass response because size requirements for enclosures vary according to the enclosure design. In order to get 20 Hz or even 30 Hz response out of an infinite baffle or horn loaded type of enclosure, enormous internal volume is required. On the other hand, a modern acoustic suspension or vented enclosure can be much smaller per a given low frequency cutoff, and the rare and costly compound type enclosures can be made smaller still. But the fact is that any loudspeaker with 30 Hz response will, of necessity, be a large, floorstanding system. No bookshelf or miniature speaker is capable of high volume, low frequency response, and immutable physical constraints will preclude such a speaker from ever being developed. If you want deep bass you'll have to live with a big speaker and that's all there is to it.

For ultimate bass response in an audio system, the consumer needs to have recourse to a special kind of loudspeaker called subwoofer. A subwoofer, as its name implies, is a speaker designed

Fig. 5-10. Thiel CS3. This unusual speaker has flat response down to 20 Hz! though the woofer is only 10 inches across. Extended frequency response is achieved by means of an outboard electronic equalizer (not shown). Note sloped front baffle for phase coherence among drivers. Courtesy of Thiel Audio Products.

exclusively for the reproduction of low bass. Most subwoofers are crossed over somewhere below 150 Hz. Typically, subwoofers are designed for response down to at least 30 Hz and often 20 Hz. A few subwoofers go down to 15 Hz, though such a specification is rare, and in any case, no compact disc and only a handful of specially cut phonograph records have musical information in this frequency range.

A subwoofer will generally add only about an octave of useful response to a speaker system, and to that extent, it appears to be something of an extravagance, but a properly integrated subwoofer can have other beneficial effects on a system than merely providing deep bass. By relieving an ordinary woofer of the obligation to reproduce any bass information below 100 Hz or so, one is sharply reducing the distortion produced by that woofer. This will greatly enhance the clarity of sounds in the lower midrange, particularly drumbeats. In my experience it is virtually impossible to reproduce the sound of a drum kit accurately without a subwoofer. Subwoofers seem particularly well suited to capturing the clean deep bass recorded on many compact discs, but they are not an investment to be made without due consideration.

Subwoofers are large and must be placed fairly close to the main speakers in order that their sound will be integrated with that of the latter. A stereo pair of subwoofers is preferable, though many records have a mono bass, and four speaker boxes in a living room can pose serious logistical problems.

Subwoofers tend to be fairly expensive in themselves, and in order to work very well, they should be powered by a separate amplifier. This, in turn, necessitates still another component called an *electronic crossover*. Some subwoofers on the market incorporate an amplifier and crossover right in the speaker box, and these tend to represent the most economical packages. Really high grade separate electronic crossovers are generally extremely expensive and choosing one that will mate well with a given combination of main speakers and subwoofers requires considerable knowledge of the principles of loudspeaker design. The separates approach in subwoofers is one that is best left to the serious hobbyist or else should be undertaken only with the consultation of a highly qualified audio retailer.

For that matter, most subwoofer, separate or self-powered, represent certain matching problems. Getting the phase relationships right between subwoofer and main speaker is always tricky, as is determining the crossover frequency. Several loudspeaker manufacturers make optional subwoofers specifically tailored for certain speakers in their lines and these completely engineered systems seem to produce the best results.

Extended treble response is easier to achieve in a loudspeaker then deep bass but most speakers on the market still exhibit a falling treble response above 10 kHz which tends to make musical instruments sound dull and lacking an impact. Speaker designers frequently tune such treble-deficient systems to produce a peak just below 10 kHz to give the impression of lively treble response. A similar trick is often used in bass deficient speakers—that is, an elevated response is engineered at a frequency just above the bass cutoff frequency. Many cheap loudspeakers exhibit both types of peaks, and hifi salesmen refer to the sound they produce as "sizzle-boom."

In addition to having limited frequency response, most speakers have several little peaks and dips within the range they do cover. Some of these may be deliberate—the familiar sizzle-boom—but others are system anomalies. The problem in achieving flat frequency response is that the drivers, the cones and domes used to produce the sound, do not themselves exhibit flat frequency response. Most speakers use two or three drivers of varying sizes, each more or less restricted to the frequency range where its own response is flattest, but this stratagem is usually insufficient to produce a completely regular frequency response. Further tuning by means of "notch filters" in the crossover network is used by many manufacturers, but that too is usually insufficient for the achievement of truly flat response.

There is no question that frequency response irregularities account for many of the "colorations" or unnatural aspects of a speaker's tonal signature. Better quality loudspeaker drivers are available today than in the past, and the finest loudspeaker systems made today certainly outperform their counterparts of 20 years ago, but frequency response remains an area of loudspeaker design in which much improvement is needed.

Now it is possible to compensate electronically for the frequency response anomalies of a loudspeaker system by means of a device called an equalizer which is a sophisticated tone control with separate adjustments for narrow frequency ranges (Fig. 5-11, 5-12). But equalizers, themselves, present several problems. First of all, they are difficult to use successfully without expensive test instruments—minimally a microphone, a spectrum analyzer, and a pink noise generator. Equalizing by ear is a maddening exercise,

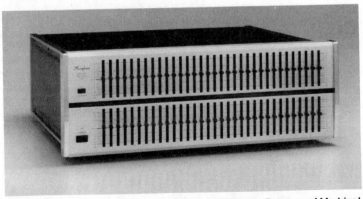

Fig. 5-11. The Accuphase 1/3 octave equalizer Cabinet. Courtesy of Madrigal Ltd.

Fig. 5-12. The circuit board for the Accuphase 1/3 octave equalizes. This component has great flexibility and uses high-quality parts and is very expensive. Courtesy of Madrigal Ltd.

and one that is simply beyond the capabilities of most listeners. Attempts to ear equalize usually result in a system with more frequency response problems than it had in the first place.

Another problem with most equalizers is their lack of precision. Most permit only broad octave adjustments, while many frequency response problems are considerably narrower than an octave. Expensive parametric and one third octave equalizers are most precise, but they're also beyond the means of most consumers.

Finally, most equalizers utilize very low quality integrated circuits and tend to add their own noise and distortions to the sound of the system. Most audio systems could probably benefit from a really high quality parametric equalizer, but so far, no one has been able to market one successfully.

In assessing the frequency response of a loudspeaker system, a distinction should be made between the response in a listening room. Most loudspeaker specifications are obtained either by testing the loudspeaker in an anechoic chamber (an acoustically "dead" room where almost no sound is reflected from the walls), or by subjecting the loudspeaker to FFT (Fast Fourier Transform) analysis in which the effects of room reflections are factored out by means of a special computer program. Such specific speaker response will be considerably altered by the acoustics of most listening rooms unless said rooms have had their walls treated with sound absorbent panels. A loudspeaker's position in a listening room may also have a major effect on frequency response, particularly bass response. Most loudspeakers tend to sound best well away from walls and especially corners.

The second major performance parameter for loudspeakers is dynamic range, and this has a considerable bearing on the speaker's suitability for compact disc reproduction. Standard speaker specs frequently don't list dynamic range. Sometimes, maximum sound pressure levels at one meter are specified, in other cases the same information can be derived by comparing efficiency and power handling capabilities. But what these figures fail to indicate is the speaker's *transfer function* or *admittance*, that is, the relationship between electrical watts of input and acoustical watts of output. Ideally, that relationship should be one to one—that is, output should be directly proportional to input. Thus, when the music signal is faint, the speaker makes faint sounds, when the music should be loud, the speaker plays loudly. Unfortunately, the transfer function is rarely as linear as it should be.

Most loudspeakers compress amplitude at either extreme, that is, they have difficulty in reproducing very faint sounds—low level detail, as it were—or in reproducing crashing crescendos. In the case of the former, they are inaudible, and in the case of the latter, they compress the signal, that is, they fail to get correspondingly louder as the strength of the input signal is rising.

A loudspeaker's transfer function is not really ascertainable from standard specs. It can only be determined by listening to the loudspeaker and there it is readily apparent to even the most untrained ear.

Small planar loudspeakers using thin membranes to produce sound (such as electrostatic loudspeakers) tend to have particularly limited dynamic range and to compress dynamics badly. Such speakers may have other virtues—they seem to be able to reproduce a lot of detail—but they won't play with much snap or impact.

Distortion is another infrequently important loudspeaker specification, though it isn't listed in most spec sheets. The majority of loudspeakers exhibit sharply rising IM distortion at playback levels exceeding 95 dB. Such distortion blurs reproduction, makes it difficult for the listener to distinguish different instruments and voices, and tends to give the speaker a harsh, fatiguing tonal quality. Small, two-way speakers having only a woofer and a tweeter and no midrange tend to be particularly prone to high distortion at relatively low listening levels. This is not to say that two-way loudspeakers are inevitably inferior to three-way speakers, as is sometimes claimed. Some of the finest speakers in the world are two-way designs, but unless a two-way loudspeaker utilizes exotic drivers with unusually wide bandwidth, it is apt to be stressed at high playback levels. Ordinary dome tweeters are difficult to operate below 2 kHz, and a 6 1/2 inch woofer, the smallest driver capable of significant response below 100 Hz, will be exhibiting rather irregular response if pushed up to 2 kHz. Any problems the drivers might have at the limits of their frequency range will be exacerbated at high volumes.

On the other hand, three-way speakers—not to mention four-ways—cost more to make due to higher parts cost and are much harder to design. Below a certain price point—say $700 a pair—three-way speakers are unlikely to use high quality parts or to exhibit high grade construction, and at such price points, two-way systems may represent a better value.

Yet another commonly cited performance specification, and one I think really is important, is *efficiency*. Efficiency in this context refers to the efficiency with which the speaker converts electrical watts into acoustical output. It is usually measured by taking the decibel level at one meter in front of the speaker on axis with an electrical input of one watt.

Most speakers play surprisingly loudly on a paltry one watt, with all but a few models ranging from between roughly 84 dB to 94 dB. 84 dB, the output for a low efficiency speaker, is still fairly loud, but remember each additional 3 dB requires a doubling of power and, thus, to get to 100 dB, assuming the speakers can handle that level, will require roughly 50 watts.

However, one should realize that efficiency measurements are invariably taken in the midrange, usually at 1 kHz, occasionally at 400 Hz. Speaker efficiency commonly dips in the bass and so, in reproducing music with heavy bass emphasis, a speaker is apt to require much more power than its rated efficiency would suggest.

All things being equal, high efficiency is clearly desirable in a loudspeaker, but all things rarely are equal. Efficient speakers typically use either horn type enclosures or high efficiency vented enclosures, and large paper cone woofers. Horn enclosures generally create a multitude of undesirable resonances and reflections, while high efficiency vented designs lack low bass and suffer from looseness and boom in the mid bass. Big paper woofers, for their part, are high in distortion and "breakup" due to spurious cone resonances. Efficiency is almost never purchased for nothing, and most of the world's most accurate loudspeakers are not high efficiency designs.

Still another frequently cited performance spec—one often included in claims of digital readiness—is power handling. Power handling is simply the ability of the speaker to absorb electrical power without being damaged. Power handling may be measured either in terms of steady state r.m.s. power, the strictest standard, or in terms of instantaneous power or "music power," a figure that is usually much higher than the former.

High power handling capacities are clearly desirable if you're aiming for high sound pressure levels and you plan to drive the speaker hard. If at all possible, you should try to get fixtures on the power handling capabilities of the individual drivers and not simply the system as a whole. That is because tweeters tend to have much lower power handling capabilities than woofers, though, paradoxically, tweeter power handling capabilities are apt to be most stressed by low powered amplifiers.

Most tweeters have continuous power handling capabilities of, at most, a few watts, which is ordinarily not much of a problem simply because real music has relatively little energy concentrated in the frequency range handled by a tweeter. But when an amplifier clips on a strong signal, the situation changes dramatically. The distortion in the signal rises significantly and since most of the distortion occurs in the upper frequency ranges, the tweeter receives a far higher energy signal that is usually the case. The result can be tweeter failure with the voice coil of the tweeter literally melting from an excessive flow of electrical current. Once that happens, the tweeter has to be replaced. One might conclude that with highly dynamic digital source materials high power handling would assume paramount importance, and, indeed, it does. But high power handling is seldom achieved without a price.

Power handling is largely a function of the ability of the electrical conductor in a loudspeaker to dissipate heat. Tweeters tend to have poor power handling abilities because relatively little conductive wire is used. Since the wire—that forms a voice coil attached to the diaphragm itself—actually moves in time with the music signal, it must be very light in weight to permit extended high frequency response. Any measure that increases voice coil mass in the interest of better heat dissipation tends to limit high frequency response, resulting in a dull-sounding treble. It's a damned if you do, damned if you don't situation.

One solution is to use two or more tweeters working in tandem. This increases the actual sound pressure level per a given signal strength and also provides a larger total surface area on the conductor to dissipate heat. Two or more tweeters with individually poor power handling may, when combined, exhibit superior power handling. But, the problem with this solution is that the cost of the speaker inevitably increases and the placement of tweeters in relationship to one another becomes extremely critical due to interference between drivers (Fig. 5-13).

Another solution—one much more commonly employed—is the use of *ferrofluid* in the magnetic gap of the loudspeaker. Ferrofluid is an electrically conductive fluid substance that greatly increases the heat dissipation of any given loudspeaker driver. Ferrofluid also alters the distribution of magnetic forces in the loudspeaker's motor assembly and makes for less predictable conversion of the electrical audio signal into electro-magnetic and ultimately electro-mechanical forces. Thus, ferrofluid represents another trade-off—decreased linearity for greater power handling.

One of the more misleading specifications applied to loudspeakers performance is dispersion or polar response. Dispersion generally refers to the ability of the loudspeaker to maintain level frequency response for off-axis listening positions. The ideal listening position for most speakers is dead center and at least eight feet back with both speakers aimed at the listener's head, any departure from that arrangement, especially one where the listener is much closer to one speaker than the other, is apt to result in the collapse of the stereo image and the appearance that the nearer speaker is producing most of the sound; however, the better the speaker's dispersion, that is, its off-axis response, the more the listener can depart from the dead center position and still get some sense of stereo (Fig. 5-14).

Dispersion problems in a loudspeaker generally grow more pronounced with ascending frequency, and high frequency sounds tend to "beam" out from the tweeter over a very narrow arc. There are many tactics that speaker designers utilize to improve dispersion but, unfortunately, most bring unwanted side effects, and, indeed,

Fig. 5-13. Polk SDA SRS. This speaker, with four tweeters per side, has enormous power handling capability. Special crossover circuitry for heightening separation between left and right speakers is included.

the desirability of good dispersion as a design goal is highly questionable in the first place (Fig. 5-15).

The stereo image formed by properly set-up loudspeakers is an illusion created by manipulating the relative intensities, phase relationships, and arrival times of sounds emanating from either speaker. Those relationships are usually predicated on a center listening position. If the individual is off center, they break down, particularly relationships of phase and arrival times. Improving dispersion can only work on the relationship of intensity and so the stereo image will, inevitably, be degraded at off center listening positions.

High dispersion designs can degrade it even more by creating an unpredictable pattern of reflections off rear and side walls, floors, and ceilings. The ear is forced to sort out multiple arrival times from amongst a multitude of reflections, and a muddled, ill-defined stereo image results. Some people like the effect, claiming that music sounds more spacious, but it clearly does violence to many kinds of recordings, particularly highly focused popular music.

Wide dispersion is achieved most commonly by using more than one high frequency element and, in some cases, by placing drivers on the back or sides of the speakers as well as in the front. Variations of this approach are used by Bose, dbx, and Acoustic Research (Fig. 5-16). Another technique is to use special drivers that radiate sound in all directions. This approach appears in speakers by Ohm,

Fig. 5-14. Dbx SF-1A Soundfield Speaker. This speaker has multiple tweeters, midranges, and woofers distributed on all sides of the cabinet to provide extremely broad dispersion. A complex crossover and equalization network balances output among drivers to improve off-axis listening and to provide some sense of stereo separation in a wide range of listening positions.

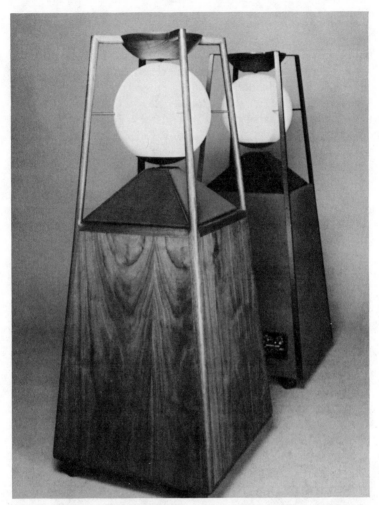

Fig. 5-15. Wolcott Audio Omnisphere. A much simpler approach to the problem of providing wide dispersion. The Omnisphere uses multiple woofers but only one tweeter that fires down over a globe shaped baffle.

Wolcott Audio, B.E.S., and Quad. It should be noted that all dipole loudspeakers, such as the Magneplanars and the Quad, and Acusthe electrostatics, radiate sound front and back and, thus, produce dispersion patterns where reflections are very prominent.

To be sure, there are many many other significant aspects of speaker performance, most of which are not subject to standard specifications. For instance, most loudspeaker drivers have a tendency to continue to radiate acoustic energy after the electrical impulse from the amplifier has passed through their electrical circuits. Thus, the loudspeaker is still transmitting the signal from a moment earlier at the same time it is handling the incoming signal. This echo from the previous instant is very faint, but it is still sufficient to blur reproduction somewhat. All loudspeakers suffer from such "overhang" as it's called, to some degree, but some are much more vulnerable than others. The loudspeaker's immunity to this defect is principally a function of driver design and quality.

Loudspeakers also suffer to varying degrees from unwanted resonances in their cabinets. In most mass produced loudspeakers, cabinet resonances reach levels of at least 20 dB below the output of the drivers, and these resonances result in blurred reproduction and a kind of "boxy" sound that lets you know you're listening to a loudspeaker and not a real performance. Cabinet resonances can be very effectively controlled by use of certain structural materials such as slate, marble, and concrete or by using a double chamber construction with a sand filling, but such tactics have never found much acceptance on the part of manufacturers due to the great weight of the resulting speaker system. The use of certain honey-

Fig. 5-16. Acoustic Research Magic Speaker. Drivers are positioned along the sides of the cabinet to create a controlled pattern of sidewall reflections to simulate concert hall ambience.

comb laminates and synthetic concretes may eventually bring about acoustically dead cabinets of reasonable weights, but for now, uncontrolled cabinet resonances remain one of the most severe problems in current production loudspeakers.

A final problem—one that is often discussed in the audio press, if not always very lucidly—is phasing problems between drivers. Such problems are caused by the crossover and by the mounting of the drivers on the front panel. All Butterworth type crossovers—the type in general use in the industry—cause phase discrepancies between drivers when the crossover roll off from driver to driver exceeds 6 dB per octave. Because 6 dB per octave is insufficient to produce good results with most drivers, manufacturers use higher rolloffs that cause progressively more phase shift. Drivers are out of sync with one another—by only a few thousandths of a second, it's true—but the phase discrepancy subtly degrades reproduction.

I could go on, but to little point. It should be apparent from this discussion that loudspeaker design still has a long way to go before perfection is achieved.

Other Components

The loudspeaker completes the signal chain, but there are a good many components called signal processors one may add to a system, most of which are inserted in the tape loop monitor of the preamp. Equalizers are the most common such signal processors, but there are many others, including dbx noise reduction modules, subsonic filters, click suppressors, ambience enhancers, and dynamic range expanders. With the exception of ambience enhancers which changes the stereo image and, of course, equalizers, nearly all of these signal processors are designed to cope with the limitations of analog storage media and so won't be of concern here.

Chapter 6

Special Features

Compact disc players currently range in price from a low of $99 (New York City discount price) up to nearly $2,000. That $2,000 maximum is likely to go up because several small American manufacturers are contemplating the marketing of machines costing not two, but several thousands of dollars. I would expect to see such machines by 1987.

A consumer facing this considerable range of prices is naturally moved to ask what extra expenditures will buy him. And his suspicions are apt to be aroused by the fact that the standard specifications for the players are nearly identical regardless of price. He's also apt to be confused by the frequent statements he encounters in the popular press that all players sound alike.

My own position is that considerable sonic differences do exist among players, and that additional expenditures do, at least in some cases, secure for the consumer better mechanical and electronic systems. At least some support for this view can be derived from the results of blind listening tests, though it must be stated that defenders of the opposite view, that players all sound alike, frequently cite listening experiments proporting to support their position.

It seems to me that any consumer contemplating the purchase of a premium player should, if at all possible, try to obtain a dealer loan of the player in question and satisfy himself that differences exist between that unit and the mass market models—differences of a sufficient magnitude to justify the additional cost. Individuals certainly vary in their sensitivity to tonal differences and, indeed, in the characteristics of musical reproduction which they deem most important. And, thus, choice of a compact disc player for its sonics will be very much an individual matter. But at the same time the consumer should be aware of those design characteristics likely to make a difference in sound quality, simply to help him narrow down the number of choices.

The consumer should also be conversant with the various convenience features on the machines because these too have a bearing on price and on value. Finally, the consumer should be aware of those details of construction that make for superior durability in a machine. Some machines on the market are obviously throwaways, while others are designed to last for years. Clearly, the projected life span for the product will be of interest to most consumers.

Each of these aspects of player quality will be considered—sonics, convenience and ease of operation, and durability; but the focus will be on the first, since sonic refinements are the least obvious and most in need of explication.

PERFORMANCE FEATURES

All compact disc players decode digital signals in fundamentally the same manner, and most players are constructed largely or entirely out of stock parts produced by a few prime manufacturers. A few basic designs predominate, and a considerable degree of uniformity characterizes the product category—far more uniformity than one will find in loudspeakers or in power amplifiers, for example. Even among players with pretensions to sonic superiority, most of the mechanical parts and electronic circuits are apt to be stock components, and, indeed, the whole machine is likely to have been assembled by a prime manufacturer with perhaps a few modifications made by the company whose brand name graces the front panel. Most of the premium machines happen to be based on Philips tray or drawer loading players, with a handful of other high end manufacturers favoring Sony decks, and fewer still choosing other brands. Sony itself makes a line of high performance machines that differ at many points from their stock machines, but Sony is virtually alone among prime manufacturers in making a premium deck from the ground up. Most high performance machines on the market are merely stock machines with a few parts substituted.

In practically all high performance machines, the loading mechanism, the motors, the optical pick-up including servos, the EFM demodulator, and the digital filter, if present, will be stock. A couple of machines have special D/A convertors and one that I know of, the ADS CD3, has a proprietary error concealment circuit. A few machines have specialized analog filters and many have unique analog amplifying circuitry. A few have built-in signal processors as well, and quite a few have redesigned power supplies. Also common in high performance decks are various forms of shock mounting and vibration damping schemes.

Perhaps the most logical way to examine performance modifications as a whole is to start with the mechanical parts of the system and then proceed through the signal path from photodiode to output buffer amp. The reader may refer back to Chapter 4 for schematics of compact disc player circuit layouts.

MECHANICAL CONSTRUCTION

On the most basic level, a heavy preponderance of metal moving parts is indicative of quality in a compact disc player and thick die cast metal parts are preferable to stamped sheet metal. A metal chassis is also preferable to a plastic cabinet in most cases. Light plastic does little to prevent airborne vibrations from loudspeakers from reaching the disc surface and laser pickup and, thus, creates tracking problems. Very extensive use of massive metal castings is made in the ADS and Revox CD players. The latter has an exceptionally heavy duty precision machined transport as well, for the Studer-Revox company is a prime manufacturer of high quality transports for tape recorders and record players (Fig. 6-1).

Fig. 6-1. Revox B225 Compact Disc Player, one of the pricier units on the market. Studer-Revox, the manufacturer, is one of the leading fabricators of high quality studio tape recorders, and the quality of Revox transports is second to none. This unit features a special heavy duty transport, four times oversampling, and all-discrete analog circuitry.

Fig. 6-2. Mission DAD 7000R. The Mission compact disc player was one of the first decks claimed to have sonics superior to the norm. Like most perfectionist decks, it is based on a Phillips four times oversampling design. Modifications include a subchassis suspension, die cast chassis, double D/A convertors, and a specially designed analog filter and buffer amp.

Unique cabinet construction techniques are also evident in the Kyocera players where a very unusual approach to suppressing unwanted vibrations has been devised. Kyocera, a world leader in industrial ceramics, encases the analog circuitry within a ceramic module and makes the entire base out of a nonresonant ceramic compound. A similar tactic has been recently adopted by Sony which makes the cabinets for its latest generation of compact disc player out of cerasin, a heavy non-resonant plastic substance.

Another resonance suppressing tactic, one used by such manufacturers as Meridian, Cambridge, and Mission, is the employment of a device known as a *subchassis* to support the transport. A subchassis is a sort of floating platform suspended on springs that isolates the moving parts of the machine in midair within the cabinet itself. Since springs are the only points of contact between the subchassis and the rest of the machine, they are also the only points at which structure-borne vibrations can impinge upon the subchassis. Because springs are not an efficient transmission line for the passage of any but low frequency vibrations, the subchassis is pretty effective at protecting the transport and optics from jolts. Subchassis have been used for years in turntables to isolate the platter and there's no question that they work (Fig. 6-2).

A different route in suspensions is taken by Yamaha which makes extensive use of rubber pads within the machine to isolate the moving parts. Rubber bushings are generally less effective in isolating mechanical systems than are subchassis, but they're a good deal easier to manufacture.

Another vibration suppressing device is the disc clamp which holds the disc firmly in contact with the platter (remember the laser eye reads the disc from the underside). Disc clamps are supplied with at least one English player, The Meridian Pro, and some listeners have been known to improvise them by placing another disc on top of the one being played.

The optics used in premium CD players are in every case stock items, and premium players have no better optical systems than standard players. Much ado is made of the presence of three-beam lasers in certain players, but as we have seen in Chapter 2, there are certain advantages to using a single beam laser. In any case, three-beam lasers are very commonly employed at all price ranges.

ELECTRONICS

As far as the actual signal circuitry goes, players are available with proprietary electronics at every stage of the signal chain with the exception of the EFM demodulator, though no player on the market has completely customized electronics.

Perhaps the rarest of proprietary circuits are specially designed error correction modules, and ADS is the only machine I know that utilizes its own unique design in this area. The ADS module is distinguished from all other error concealment circuits by the presence of a variable *window*. The term window refers to the number of bits that is held by the circuit at any one time, used for computing average values in order to reconstruct missing bits, and by extension, missing portions of the wave form encoded in the bit stream. In any error concealment scheme the wider the window, the more information the circuit has to work with, and the more likely the machine can quickly locate sync bits and lock back onto the track when a break is present due to dirt, abrasions, etc. Unfortunately, widening the window also increases the susceptibility of the system to jitter (a term for minor mistracking due to minute variations in the speed of rotation), as well as to defocusing of the laser pickup; while a narrow window aids the operation of the CIRC demodulator. ADS attempts to have the best of both worlds by changing the window aperture according to the presence or absence of errors—widening the window to locate sync bits when extensive amounts of data have been destroyed, and narrowing it under normal conditions (Fig. 6-3).

The next stages in the signal path, digital filtering and D/A conversion, are generally agreed to have a major effect on the quality of reproduction and have been subjected to a number of refinements in several of the more sophisticated machines.

First, it should be said that of the premium machines currently on the market all, save for the Luxman DO3, use oversampling and

Fig. 6-3. ADS CD3. The ADS compact disc player features heavy die cast chassis, a proprietary error correction scheme, and a highly unusual filter described in detail in the text. Unlike most perfectionist players, the ADS is based on the Sony deck.

digital filtering (described in Chapter 4). Something near to a consensus has grown up among subjective reviewers that the phase shift and group delay engendered by steep filters is sonically undesirable and should be avoided. Nevertheless, it should also be noted that the greater phase linearity brought about by digital filtering schemes is not obtained without a price. The price is a net increase in the amount of high frequency spuriae that ultimately must be suppressed. The initial 44.1 kHz sampling frequency, or "clock," is entirely removed from the signal itself by digital filtering, but before that process is completed, this high frequency signal has reacted with the power supply and possibly radiated over to the analog circuitry, depending on how well the analog circuitry has been shielded. To be sure, all compact discs have current regulation to minimize the effects of the clock, and some players have separate power supplies feeding the digital and analog circuits to further minimize clock interference, but, where a single supply is used, the power supply does provide a pathway where clock frequencies can migrate from one circuit to another, in effect bypassing the filtering system (Fig. 6-4).

Worse still, in most digital filtering systems, up to four additional clocks are created during the oversampling process. Such clock frequencies are filtered out within the signal path itself, but they still may radiate through the power supply, through the electrical grounds, or through the chassis. Mindful of this problem, Sony Corporation has recently introduced a revision of its two times oversampling system in which a single master clock frequency is used to synchronize all digital decoding functions. With Sony's system only one high frequency clock is present (Fig. 6-5).

In most decks using the Philips four times oversampling sys-

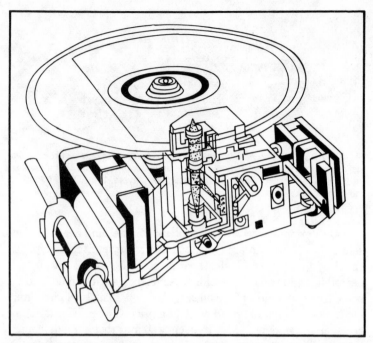

Fig. 6-4. Sony's new linear torque motor, said to offer better speed regulation than competing units. Courtesy of Sony Corporation.

tem, the D/A convertor is provided with only 14-bit resolution; in other words, two bits less than the stated resolution of the medium. This would ordinarily translate into 12 dB more noise and 12 dB less dynamic range, but the actual output of the circuit was claimed by Philips to have 16-bit accuracy. Whether this is true is a matter of debate among engineers. In systems using the 14-bit D/A convertor, the convertor itself is preceded by a noise shaping circuit that achieves 6 dB noise reduction by digital manipulation of the signal. Another 6 dB of noise suppression is gained by the over-

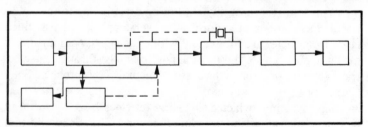

Fig. 6-5. Block diagram of Sony masterclock system. Courtesy of Sony Corporation.

sampling itself since some of the noise is distributed among the ultrasonic frequencies that are removed by the digital filter. The actual signal to noise level of players using this circuit is, thus, the same as that of a player without oversampling which employs the 44.1 kHz D/A convertor.

Nevertheless, several manufacturers maintain that true 16-bit resolution is preferable in a four times oversampling machine, and they have provided it. The first to do so was a small English electronics company named Cambridge Audio. Cambridge brought out a 16 bit player in 1985 (presently no longer distributed in this country) that utilized not one, but three 16-bit D/A convertors (actual resolution is 19 or 20 bits, but system resolution cannot exceed 16). The three convertors operate together and the outputs of all are pooled or averaged to reduce error. Each individual convertor is fabricated out of several lower resolution chips because a single cost effective low noise 16-bit convertor designed to operate at 176.4 kHz (the requisite clock frequency for four times oversampling) simply wasn't available at the time the player was introduced. Subsequently, Philips and one or two other manufacturers have produced commercial versions of such chips and today two other four times oversampling players, the Kyocera 9A-910 and the Tandberg 3015A, operate at true 16-bit resolution.

A more common refinement involving D/A convertors is to use two of them—one for each stereo channel. The advantage of this ploy is that the two stereo channels may be routed to their respective amplifier inputs at precisely the same instant. When only one D/A convertor is used, the right hand channel outputs are out of sync by 11 microseconds, a seemingly insignificant amount, but still the presence of such delays has been detected in blind listening tests, and standard design principles would dictate the superiority of dual filters over just one. It should be noted that not all double D/A convertor players maintain perfect phase relations between channels, but the use of double convertors facilitates correct phasing.

Quite a few of the better players on the market have separate power supplies for analog and digital section and more have a separate supply for the motor and servo mechanisms that guide the pickup. We have already touched upon the problems of leakage of clock frequencies from the digital section into the analog circuitry of the player. Electrical noise from the motors could be even more sonically disastrous. The presence of motor noise and clock frequencies is not apt to show up on a standard test for harmonic distortion, but such high frequency spuriae could certainly create intermodulation distortion if allowed to enter analog circuits.

Single point star grounding arrangement combined with heavy copper grounding strips also appear on a number of players including the PS Audio CD-1 and the Luxman DO3. Extensive use of non-magnetic chassis materials such as aluminum is another tactic for preventing the leakage of digital clock frequencies into analog sections. This kind of engineering practice has long characterized high quality preamplifiers and amplifiers, but it seems to me that it is needed much more in a compact disc player due to the presence of relatively intense bursts of high frequency energy that are unrelated to the music signal itself. The Kyocera and Meridian players are both characterized by extensive magnetic shielding.

Following the D/A convertor, we have the output sample and hold or aperture circuit, and the analog filter. The aperture circuit, as a rule, is a stock component and has not been the focus of much engineering effort on the part of perfectionist designers. The analog filter is a different story, however. A great many premium machines have specially designed output filters, for the filter itself constitutes an obvious weak link in the whole system.

Analog filters are problematic for a number of reasons. As seen, they characteristically introduce phase shift and distortion. Phase shift is worst for the type of filter known as a Butterworth, the standard topology for loudspeaker crossovers; consequently, the Butterworth is never used in compact disc players. Instead, more phase coherent types—the Bessel or the Chebyschev—are employed although both of these types achieve superior phase response only at the expense of introducing slight frequency response irregularities. In complex filters it is possible to juggle the values of phase and frequency response to achieve the best balance for a given system, and it is also possible to incorporate phase and amplitude correcting networks to undo some of the damage caused by the filter. Generally, in the perfectionist players, phase will be optimized at the slight expense of frequency response on the theory that any minor frequency anomalies in the last octave above 10 kHz will not be very perceptible.

One particularly interesting output filter appears on the ADS CD3. Practically all such filters are centered around 20 kHz, the stated limit of CD frequency response, but the ADS filter begins to attenuate frequency response only in the region above 35 kHz, thus leaving a region from 20 kHz to 35 kHz essentially unfiltered. The digital filter should have removed most of the high frequency energy in this area anyway, and the higher "knee" frequency for the filter itself will result in less phase shift within the audible bandwidth. Recently, Shure Brothers in their D5000 player have adopted a similar type of filter.

In order for filters to perform their function consistently over the months and years, they must be made of high quality capacitors and resistors, and parts quality is one area where premium machines may be expected to differ from mass market products. We would expect that in output filters using less than optimal electrical components, the electrical values of those components would begin to drift within months of use and the effects of such drift would be difficult to predict. The slope or steepness of the filter would stay pretty much the same, but some subtle degradations in sound might manifest themselves, particularly in the machine's ability to reproduce transient attacks. A great deal of debate has occurred in audio engineering circles in recent years on the audibility of capacitor and resistor differences, although a consensus is growing among perfectionist designers that capacitor quality does make a difference in an analog circuit.

A few players, such as the Cambridge, have selectable output filters to compensate for the varying degrees of phase shift and preemphasis caused by the different antialiasing filters in use on professional digital mastering tape recorders. Such a multifilter output stage is an expensive option and I doubt that it will appear on many players. Interestingly, a somewhat similar type of phase compensation is present in the CD input section of the Krell PAM-3 preamplifier. Selectable filtering is present here also, but it is designed to improve upon the filters in specific makes of players rather than to address the phase irregularities of the master tape.

The analog buffer amplifier that forms the last stage of the signal chain in compact disc players has, somewhat ironically, been the area that has most exercised designers seeking to improve the sound of the players. Ordinarily, this buffer stage is extremely simple, utilizing only a couple of transistors to amplify the voltage of the now analog signal. The little voltage amplifier will be accompanied by various other circuit elements for adjusting the operating bias of the gain transistor and for regulating the electrical current which it draws from the power supply; occasionally an attenuator (volume control) will be placed after this stage to permit direct coupling of the CD player with the power amplifier. Generally, all of these elements will be etched onto a single integrated circuit—a chip as it were—and such chips can be purchased from electronic suppliers for literally pennies. Similar chips are also used in the output stages of cassette decks and tuners, and they are sometimes—not always accurately—referred to as op amps.

Most buffer ICs use rather imprecise, high distortion gain transistors and very high values of feedback to get the distortion down. While the effects of heavy feedback on a single stage as opposed to a whole amplifier circuit are probably a good deal less detrimental, a conviction has arisen among many designers that better results can be obtained from a custom designed analog circuit using discrete parts than from an off-the-shelf IC.

In 1984, Meridian, a small English electronics manufacturer, introduced a CD player with a discrete buffer amp that immediately won plaudits from many prominent subjective reviewers. Meridian's example was followed by a host of manufacturers including Mission, Kyocera, PS Audio, Distech, Kinegetics, Tandberg, and others. The culmination of this trend appears to have been reached recently by the announcements by Distech Corporation and a new company called California Audio Labs that each would be introducing a compact disc player with a vacuum tube buffer amp (Fig. 6-6).

Vacuum tubes, it should be known, are still favored by many audio enthusiasts for use in voltage amplification, and it is perhaps inevitable that someone would advocate tubes in an "ultimate" CD player. I haven't heard either player, both of which exist only in prototype at the time of this writing, but I must confess to a degree of skepticism. With only one amplification stage in the CD player itself as compared to perhaps four or five for the rest of the audio system, and given the fact that tube amplification is inher-

Fig. 6-6. Discrete Technology Compact Disc Player. Discrete Technology, Distech for short, is primarily a manufacturer of high quality interconnect cables. Their CD player is wired with this cable and is equipped with discrete analog circuitry, heavy duty power supplies, and special filtering. Supposedly the D/A convertor is custom-made. Courtesy of Distech.

Fig. 6-7. Dbx DX3 Compact Disc Player. Extensively described in the text. Courtesy of dbx.

ently noisier than solid state, especially at low voltage levels, I question the utility of tubes for CD players, even in perfectionist applications. But, as I say, I haven't heard a CD player using tubes, so I must reserve judgment.

A few compact disc players have additional circuitry immediately before or after the buffer amp for the purpose of processing the signal. Such onboard signal processors are proprietary circuits supposedly conceived to correct for deficiencies in the recordings but included, I think, primarily to differentiate the players incorporating such a circuit from the great masses of me-too players on the market (more than 50 companies currently market compact disc players, although only a handful make all or part of the players bearing their names).

The dbx DX3 is perhaps the most generously equipped of these hotrodded CD players, featuring as it does an ambience enhancing circuit, a compressor, and a dynamic range expander (Fig. 6-7). Ordinarily, one would tend to regard such accessories as so much gimmickry, but dbx, as a company, has extensive experience in manufacturing signal processors for the recording industry, and their circuits are a little more sophisticated than the norm for consumer products. They are worth at least a brief description since two of them address problems that have also exercised the two other manufacturers making signal processor CD players.

The compressor circuit in the dbx has the effect of reducing the level of very loud passages. The circuit, dubbed "Over-Easy" compression by dbx, operates by muting signals very gradually as their decibel level rises, where most compressors cut in rather abruptly squashing dynamics in music and robbing it of impact. The dbx compressor is adjustable so that degree of compression can be varied considerably according to the needs of the consumer.

One may argue that a compressor defeats the whole purpose of digital recording which is to increase dynamic range and to avoid compression of peaks, but in practical terms, a compressor serves a purpose. If compact discs are to be used as background music, a limited dynamic range may be desirable, and if they are to be recorded onto cassettes for use in portable applications, limiting dynamic range may be necessary to prevent tape overload. Such a compressor circuit would be even more applicable in an automotive CD player, but so far no one has marketed such a device.

The dbx DX3's second signal processor, the dynamic range expander, has almost the opposite effect. It actually increases the dynamic range of compact discs to an incredible 106 dB. The circuit is not really intended to make loud sounds louder; instead, it is designed to sharpen transients—more particularly the leading edges of instrumental sounds known as "attacks." Dbx advises that the circuit is only likely to produce audible benefit when used with CDs that have been made from analog masters. That is because conventional analog tape recorders have a tendency to smear attacks due to certain effects produced by the magnetic field created by the recording head. The dbx circuit senses the rapid accelerations in voltage gain that represent attacks, and pumps up the sound level for the merest fraction of a second. Similar circuits have been used for increasing the impact of phonograph records for years, but the dbx is probably the most sophisticated. Undoubtedly, some recordings benefit from the dbx treatment, especially popular recordings that have been extensively "mixed down," since each analog transfer blunts transients a little more.

The final dbx circuit is an ambience enhancer—simply a circuit that blends stereo right and left channels together. The effect of the circuit is to reduce stereo separation, and the circuit permits a broad range of adjustments between maximum separation (90 dB) and something very close to monaural. One might be moved to ask the purpose of such a feature, for high separation is generally considered one of the virtues of the compact disc format. The answer is somewhat surprising: many listeners actually prefer limited separation on the order of 20 dB or so. Reduced separation in a stereo recording, particularly if accompanied by slight phase discrepancies between channels, provides many listeners with an illusion of hall ambience—that is, reflected sound—and seems to produce a more solid phantom center image between the two speakers. If nothing else, the circuit makes compact discs sound more like phonograph records and certain listeners prefer the familiar sound of phonograph reproductions, with their relatively limited separation, to the wide separation of compact discs.

The Carver Digital Time Lens, available either as an outboard device or as an integral circuit in the Carver Compact Disc player, also affects separation when reproducing compact discs; but the Carver circuit involves substantially more signal processing than the dbx ambience enhancer, and alters the frequency response of the signal as well (Fig. 6-8). The time lens matrixes the stereo signals much in the manner of an FM modulator in a radio transmitter, then produces sum (left plus right) and difference (left minus right) signals, and then demodulates sum and difference back into simple left and right. Before demodulation, the time lens boosts the difference signal (left minus right) which carries a component of reflected sound in many recordings, particularly classical recordings done in concert halls. The circuit also provides for equalization to more closely approximate the frequency balance of a typical LP as compared to a CD. A cut in the mid treble and a boost in the mid bass will bring CDs back into a balance according to Carver Corporation. This equalization is done before demodulation to both the sum and difference signals, and to compensate for phase shifts between the signals caused by equalization, a phase correcting network is also incorporated into the Time Lens.

Perhaps the most unusual and controversial error correction circuits are incorporated in the Kinergetics KCD-1. Kinergetics is a small Los Angeles-area electronics company that has specialized in the development of correction circuits for various audio components including amplifiers, loudspeakers, phono cartridges, and tape

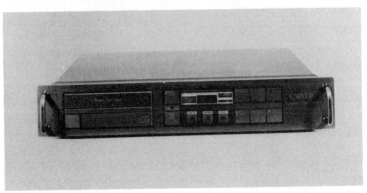

Fig. 6-8. Carver Compact Disc Player with Digital Time Lens. Extensively described in the text. Courtesy of Carver Corporation.

recorders. Their compact disc players incorporate two of the correction circuits the company has previously developed, one for amplifiers and another for tape recorders. If that sounds a little out of place in a CD player, read on.

Kinergetics is a company with an ideology. The ideology is based on a belief that "hysteretic" effects are responsible for most of the audible anomalies in solid state electronic components. The term hysteresis generally refers to the lag that occurs between the time electrical current flows through a circuit and the time when a magnetic field forms in response to that current flow, or vice versa. Kinergetics uses the term analogously to refer to lags in the turn on behavior of transistors as well as to lags that are truly hysteretic such as those in magnetic phono cartridges and magnetic recording heads.

One correction circuit devised by the company removes the purported hysteretic effects from the output amplifier on the CD player. Another, which is switchable, is supposed to compensate for the hysteresis in the analog master tape of analog mastered CDs. In my very limited experience with the player I heard no difference as a result of the analog tape circuit, and I am frankly dubious about the utility of the correction circuit for the output amp; however, the player itself does have a number of other performance features that might justify its price, including all discrete analog circuitry, separate heavy duty power supply, vibration damping, etc.

And that about sums up the major sonic refinements available on consumer compact disc players. The above descriptions do not exhaust a discussion of compact disc features, however, because the compact disc player is, above all, a convenience medium and convenience features abound on current generation players.

CONVENIENCE FEATURES

Let's start with the most fundamental convenience features and ascend by degrees through increasing levels of complexity.

To begin with, all compact disc players are automatic in the sense that the laser pickup automatically cues itself when you press the play button. The laser pickup is motor-driven, so automatic cueing comes as a matter of course.

All compact disc players are further automated to the extent that selections can be automatically accessed by front panel or remote controls. Since there is no practical way to cue by eye due to the fact that the disc is concealed in play and the tracks are invisible in any case, one has to be able to access selections by means of automated controls. All players, without exception, have such controls.

In addition, horizontal front loading CD players, which include the majority of players currently on the market, generally have controls for power loading, that is, for automatically sliding the disc tray in and out of the machine.

Most compact disc players, excluding all but the very cheapest and a few perfectionist machines with an emphasis on sonics, are programmable to varying degrees. Generally, programming will be done by means of a handheld infrared remote. The remote comes equipped with a program button and a numerical keypad on which one enters the numbers of the selections in the order that one wishes to here them.

More fully automated players have a feature called "self program search" whereby the user can skip forward and backward at will, arriving always at the beginning of succeeding or preceding tracks. A more sophisticated variant is known as "disc scanning." Here the automatic search process provides the user with brief samples of the music for a particular track. Following the conclusion of the sample, the laser pickup will advance 30 seconds into the selection and play another brief sample. Why would one wish such a feature? That is a question best left to Japanese industrial designers.

Many compact disc players have memory functions as well, enabling the user to store commands. One such command that is possible with many players is memory stop. This is almost like a tab on a typewriter keyboard. One marks a location—any location—on a disc and by use of the fast forward or fast backward control, one can access that location almost instantly.

Most players have digital displays on the front panel indicating program time elapsed to the second, and, in many cases, the number of the selection being played. The subcode information on the disc itself makes such displays extremely easy to implement (Fig. 6-9).

Perhaps the ultimate convenience feature on a compact disc player is multiplay capability, in other words, provision for playing more than one disc. In fact, several CD "changers" are currently offered by such manufacturers as Nikko, Sony, and Mitsubishi; and the Nikko NCD-600, the largest of the lot, holds up to 60 discs—a veritable CD jukebox. Given the small size of the compact disc and its superior resistance to surface abrasions, automatic loading and unloading are fairly easily effected, and, un-

131

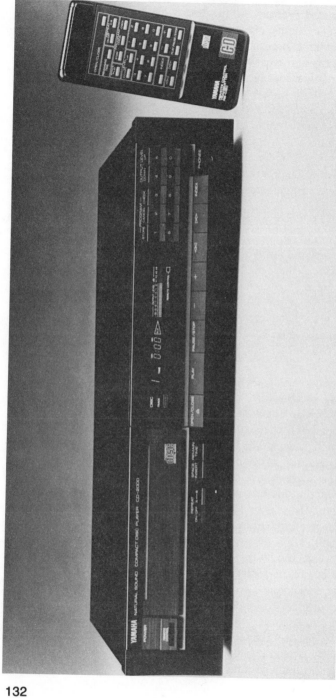

Fig. 6-9. Yamaha CD 2000 Compact Disc Player. Yamaha decks are two times oversampling designs with proprietary digital electronics and extensive resonance suppressing measures. Courtesy of Yamaha Electronics.

like the record changer, its CD counterpart need not degrade sound quality. The CD changer is the ultimate background music system, and I expect it to become commonplace not only in domestic installations but in commercial establishments where "canned music" is considered a necessity.

Auxiliary Outputs

The compact disc format, as indicated in Chapter 4, has sufficient storage capacity to permit the inclusion of still picture programming, and a few players on the market have a special video output for linking the deck with a video monitor. Thus far, at least in the United States, there is an absence of software.

At least one component, the Sony DAS-702ES, has a digital port that permits the digitized signal to be transmitted out of the deck to a digital preamplifier thereby bypassing the D/A convertor. The DAS-702ES is a unique component, an outboard D/A convertor that docks with the top of the line Sony CDP-650ESD as well as with professional tape recorders, and as yet unreleased formats such as DAT and DBS satellite. No digital preamp is currently on the market in the U.S. to accept the output of the DAS-702ES, although Sansui has introduced one in Japan—actually part of an integrated amplifier featuring pulse width modulation at the power stage.

THE PURCHASING DECISION

Fewer differences exist among compact disc players than among most other categories of audio components. Cassette decks and turntable-tonearm-cartridge combinations exhibit gross differences in frequency response and pitch accuracy but few CD players are distinguishable by such tonal characteristics, although cheaply made CD players seem to be distinguished from the better designed units by a tendency toward harshness in high frequency reproduction and an inability to suggest ambience or faint reverberation. This is a purely personal observation, but similar impressions have been recorded by members of the audio press throughout the world. Such sonic limitations are of little importance in reproducing most popular music and are likely to seem serious as limitations only with classical selections.

In purchasing a compact disc player, as in purchasing any other audio component, you will do best if you come armed to the audio showroom with a selection of discs containing music that you appreciate and with which you are familiar. Try to audition two or more compact disc players on an A-B back and forth basis. Most preamps have enough auxiliary inputs so that at least three players can be hooked up and you can easily switch between and among them from the front panel of the preamp. If great differences exist for you they should become evident in this situation. You might want a friend present to switch among players without identifying them to determine if you can reliably select among players on the basis of blind listening. Don't spend money on differences you can't hear. If a cheaper model meets your needs, go with the cheaper model provided mechanical construction is sound. As indicated, metal moving parts are preferable, because plastics have a limited life span when exposed to the constant heat of laser pickups and high voltage circuits.

A final note: I see no evidence that players will undergo any fundamental improvements within the next three to five years. Standards have been fixed and the medium is essentially mature. The only thing the consumer can look forward to is rising prices due to dollar devaluation.

Chapter 7

Automotive and
Portable Applications

The compact disc was intended to be a universal medium with applications in broadcast, domestic audio system, automotive stereo systems, and handheld portables. The small size of the compact disc permits the construction of players only a little larger than a miniature cassette recorder and, amazingly, the labyrinthine circuitry of the players can be crammed into a few large scale integrated circuits not much bigger than a half a handful of aspirin tablets. Such miniaturization makes portable versions of the machines a very reasonable proposition. Miniaturizing the operating parts of the compact disc players presented few fundamental design problems, but protecting those parts from shock and vibration in portable applications proved much more difficult.

The first automotive compact disc players showed themselves to be relatively prone to mistracking, and the Discman type of portable CD player can probably never be made to yield a really high fidelity signal due to the continual shocks it must endure as the user jogs along with it.

In the two years since the first automotive players were shown, manufacturers of the machines have devoted a tremendous amount of effort to develop effective vibration damping, and the best of the current automotive CD players are pretty effectively shielded from all but the most intense road-generated shocks and, consequently, almost never mistrack audibly. Nevertheless, we may speculate that a subtle degradation due to minor mistracking does

Fig. 7-1. Alpine Model 7900 combination FM/AM Tuner and Compact Disc Player, one of the most popular units made. Courtesy of Alpine-Luxman.

occur, and that the sheer delicacy of the pickup mechanism virtually precludes the same level of reproduction possible in the home. Then, too, no automotive CD player boasts the circuit refinements available in the better house machines. Automotive CD players, by and large, are equivalent to first generation domestic products. They are likely to remain that way (Fig. 7-1).

DIGITAL SOUND COMES TO THE AUTOMOBILE

The first automotive compact disc players were introduced in late 1984, a little over a year after the format appeared in the home. The debut players were manufactured by Sony and Pioneer, who are still the dominant prime manufacturers today. Prices were high at first—in excess of $500—and availability was very limited, but by the end of 1985, automotive compact disc players were selling about as well as equivalently priced cassette decks for the car. In 1986, compact disc players began to be offered by automotive manufacturers as factory options, and all of the major American auto manufacturers have committed to the new format.

An automotive compact disc player is essentially similar to a home unit, but the transport mechanism is miniaturized, and a special switching power supply, similar to those used in microcomputers, is used to boost the 12-volt electrical current from the battery to the high voltages needed for the digital circuitry. The players include a preamplifier, and the output is fed directly to a power amplifier.

All automotive compact disc players are two-part systems; that is, separate chassis house the electronics and the mechanical parts. All players contain shock absorbers of a sort as well, to shield the mechanical transport from jolts and vibration. A few models include AM-   radios in the same chassis housing as the player transport.

136

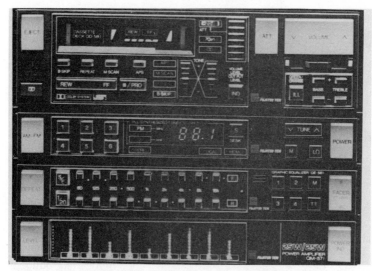

Fig. 7-2. Fujitsu Compo 581 System. Courtesy Fujitsu Ten.

None includes cassette decks (Figs. 7-2, 7-3).

Automotive compact disc players boast essentially the same specifications as home units, including more than 90 dB of dynamic range. All automotive compact disc players, with the exception of the Mitsubishi model, must be used with outboard power amplifiers, the more powerful the better. Because most automotive audio systems are build around a cassette receiver that includes a low powered amplifier of no more than 25 watts, the purchase of a CD player for the car will generally involve a costly upgrade including the purchase of an amp and quite possibly new speakers that can handle the increased dynamic range.

For those unfamiliar with automotive audio systems in general, it should be recognized that the norm is pretty low fidelity com-

Fig. 7-3. The optional SD-1110 Compact Disc Player for Fujitsu is a pricey, high-power, off-the-shelf integrated audio system from a company not previously known for high end products. This whole ensemble takes up considerable space on the dashboard. Courtesy of Fujitsu Ten.

pared to what is generally available in the home, and generally not up to the task of reproducing digital audio. Few of the off-the-shelf coaxial and plate loudspeakers, that fit in standard cutouts or mount on doors or against body panels, have significant bass response below 100 Hz, and many car amplifiers made today produce several percent harmonic distortions when the norm for home products is well below one percent. Obtaining loudspeakers with usable re-

Fig. 7-4. An elaborate custom installation built around a Sony CD player.

sponse below 50 Hz almost always involves an extensive installation in which speakers are actually built into the trunk or a specially prepared speaker box is contoured to fit the car's interior (Figs. 7-4, 7-5).

A detailed discussion of automotive audio systems isn't possible in a book of this scope, but an overview of general systems requirements for compact disc players would not be amiss and with it some observations concerning the products and services available to assemble a truly digital-ready autosound system.

The Player

Currently, all automotive compact disc players, whatever the brand designation, are actually fabricated by only three prime manufacturers, Sony, Pioneer, and Mitsubishi. Most of the players on the market are made by Sony, though a number of companies buying the Sony players, such as Alpine and Yamaha, actually do modify the basic Sony decks to their own specifications. Sony-made decks generally have a better reputation for immunity to mistracking than the Pioneer machines, and in any case, Pioneer decks are poorly distributed. Mitsubishi decks are more poorly distributed still, though interestingly the Mitsubishi machines were the first automotive products to use the over-sampling scheme favored by most perfectionist manufacturers of home CD players (Figs. 7-6, 7-7).

Of the currently available models, two decks are especially noteworthy, the Yamaha YCD-1000 and the Sony Disc Jockey. The first features unique protective sleeves for storing CDs in the car. The discs are loaded into the machine while still in the sleeves, and the laser pickup reads the information on the discs through a slot in the sleeve. The sleeves are basically similar to those used with the obsolete CED videodisc format. I believe that such sleeves represent an excellent concept. Removing a compact disc from its "jewelbox" container is difficult to accomplish with one hand while driving, and to perform the action two handed is, of course, rather hazardous. And yet, to leave the discs exposed on a seat is to risk damage to the discs. The Yamaha approach is an ingenious solution to a real problem (Fig. 7-8).

The Sony Disc Jockey solves the same problem by making disc selection and loading automatic. The Disc Jockey is essentially a CD jukebox or changer. Up to ten compact discs may be loaded into a hopper and the user may play selections from them in any

Fig. 7-5. Note multiple amplifiers, elaborate control electronics, and two woofers—all mounted in the trunk. This impeccable installation was done by Sound Plus Wood in Boca Raton, Florida, a leading east coast custom installation. Courtesy of Sound Plus Wood.

140

Fig. 7-6. Another elaborate custom installation with Alpine Compact Disc Player—this one from Speakerworks of Orange, California, a premier west coast custom installer. The car is a 1985 Thunderbird.

order. The Disc Jockey will ordinarily be mounted in the trunk and controlled by the user from the front panel. It is fully programmable and selections can be preselected and played automatically (Fig. 7-9).

The Electronics

An automotive audio system is somewhat different from its

Fig. 7-7. Compare this installation with the Ford factory compact disc system. Courtesy of Speakerworks.

Fig. 7-8. Yamaha YCD Car CD Player with Yamaha protective CD cartridge. Courtesy of Yamaha.

domestic counterpart. First of all, a separate component preamp is a rarity. Both compact disc players and cassette tuners have line amps built in and most systems utilize the line amp in the headpiece.

Secondly, an outboard power amplifier is a necessity in any serious system, especially one incorporating a compact disc player (Fig. 7-10). There are no high power receivers for the car, and no provisions on receivers for accepting input from a CD player. Spar-

Fig. 7-9. Ford-JBL system. This is the most elaborate factory audio system ever made, and the first American system to include a compact disc player as an option. Courtesy of Ford Motor Company.

komatic makes an adaptor for routing the output of a portable CD player through the antenna lead of a receiver, but that strikes me as a makeshift and the process of FM modulating the CD output certainly degrades the sound. If you want to get any measure of performance out of an automotive CD player, you need an amplifier.

Automotive power amplifiers are often optimistically or misleadingly rated for power compared to home units, and you should pay close attention to power specs for that reason. Make sure you're clear as to whether the rating is for total watts, that is, both channels combined, or for watts per channel. Home amps are virtually always rated for watts per channel and, thus, a hundred watt amp will have a total wattage of 200 watts. Car amps are more commonly rated for total wattage, which makes them sound more impressive.

Automotive amps are virtually always rated for power into four rather than eight ohms (the home standard) because virtually all automotive speakers are nominally four ohms. Very few automotive amps can drive the two ohm loads presented by two pairs of speakers in parallel. In other words, automotive amps are generally run at the ragged edge of their current limitations.

Some automotive amplifiers are rated for maximum power at a ten percent distortion figure which is well into the clipping region. Accordingly, you should check spec sheets carefully to make sure that full power is rated at distortion figures below one percent. Amplifiers by such manufacturers as Alpine, Kenwood, Concord, Hifonics, and Nakamichi are conservatively rated and will

Fig. 7-10. Alphasonik 40 watt per channel amplifier. A high power outboard amplifier is practically a necessity with a compact disc player in a car. Courtesy of Alphasonik.

make full power at low levels of distortion.

The practice of bi or triamplification, which is rare in the home, is very common in component automotive stereo systems and should be seriously considered in a compact disc-based system. The utilization of multiple amplifiers makes more efficient use of electrical power than a single amp equivalent to the combined power ratings of the two or three amps used in a bi or triamp amp system. Biamplification also offers more protection to tweeter elements from the adverse effects of clipping.

As in a domestic audio system, a biamped automotive system requires an electronic crossover, which constitutes a considerable added expense. Generally, in a biamped system you can figure on spending well over $500 on electronics alone.

Speakers

Compact discs can place considerable demands on loudspeakers, and most off-the-shelf speakers aren't really up to those demands. As with amplifiers, the printed specifications tend toward inflated claims.

Automotive loudspeakers are subject to the same basic physical constraints as home speakers. Bass response and efficiency are limited by the size of the woofers, and the enclosure space behind them. Twelve and even 15 inch woofers are available for automotive applications, but few cars have the space for mounting such monsters, at least not without extensive customizing. Consequently, normal automotive loudspeakers rarely use drivers exceeding eight inches across, and three and one half inches to six and one half inches is the more usual range.

Adequate enclosure volume for deep bass would, at first glance, appear even more difficult to achieve in a car than adequate woofer size, but in cars having a trunk, the trunk itself may be used as an enclosure simply by mounting woofers in the rear deck or under the seat. In cars without a trunk, the woofers may either be "flush mounted" on interior surfaces, in which case a scant few cubic inches of enclosure volume will be attainable, or else small box speakers may be used. These may be either custom-made to harmonize with the car's interior, or selected off-the-shelf and mounted on brackets or swivels—generally somewhere in the rear.

Flush mounted loudspeakers for the car usually have negligible bass response below 100 Hz. Small swivel-mounted box speakers will generally go slightly lower. Trunk mounted woofers will produce the lowest bass of all because the average trunk forms a very large enclosure indeed, but the bass is apt to be loose and boomy due to uncontrolled resonances in the trunk itself. The best bass response in a car is obtained by building a speaker box into the trunk, a favorite trick of custom installers.

Most high performance automotive loudspeaker systems assume a "satellite-subwoofer" configuration. A pair or more of small two-way speakers with tweeters and combination midrange woofers will be placed somewhere in the car where they will project more or less directly at the listener's head (most autosound systems are optimized for a single listener—the driver). In addition, a number of subwoofers will be installed generally in the back of the vehicle— either in custom-made enclosures, or on the rear deck with the backs of the drivers loaded into the trunk. In most, but not all, such systems, the subwoofer will be driven by a separate high-powered amplifier.

Satellite-subwoofer systems were formerly offered exclusively by custom installers, but recently Ford Motor Company has made available such a system with optional compact disc player on a few luxury vehicles. It seems likely that such systems will be offered by increasing numbers of auto manufacturers in the future.

PORTABLE AND PERSONAL COMPACT DISC PLAYERS

Compact disc players of very small dimensions are currently available in portable formats. Sony has a highly successful "Discman" player weighing just a few ounces and provided with lightweight headphones. The unit has proved very popular with joggers even at a $300 retail list price (Fig. 7-11).

Many companies currently offer compact disc players as parts

Fig. 7-11. Sony Discman portable CD player. Courtesy of Sony Corporation.

Fig. 7-12. Sony CD-5 compact disk boombox. Includes AM/FM tuner, equalizer, and cassette deck as well as CD player.

of the portable stereos known as "boom boxes" or "musical suit-cases." These are handheld units generally consisting of a radio, cassette player, amplifier and speakers as well as a compact disc player (Fig. 7-12). In view of the relatively low fidelity of amplifier and the loudspeaker I would question the sonic benefits that the compact disc would bring to such a format. Though, of course, the

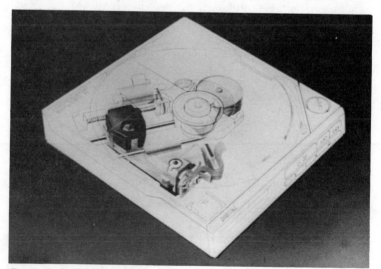

Fig. 7-13. Sony D-5 portable compact disc player.

compact disc does have the benefit of permanence in portable as well as ordinary domestic applications.

Portable players, themselves, might not be so permanent. The transports, themselves, are principally made of plastic, and subjected as they are to the heat generated by the laser pickup, they may not endure years of frequent use (Fig. 7-13). But with prices continually descending, that might not matter. In the future, expect to see prices for portables as low as $100.

Chapter 8

Other Digital Audio Media and Components for Consumer Use

The compact disc has had by far the greatest impact of any development in digital audio to date, but it is by no means the only digital audio system available to the public, nor was it even the first such consumer system. Digital audio circuits of various sorts have been appearing in consumer products since the early 1970s and will surely appear much more frequently in the future. While it is rather unlikely that analog audio circuitry will be entirely supplanted by digital any time within the century, digital circuits will be increasingly used in amplifiers, preamplifiers, radios, and signal processors, as well as in digital recording media apart from the compact disc.

Perhaps the easiest way to survey available digital audio technologies for the home is to proceed along the signal path from source to loudspeaker. Digital circuits have been developed for virtually every electronic component used in home audio, and digital speakers of a sort have even been produced experimentally. The theoretical advantages of no-loss digital transmission recommend the use of digital circuits at all points in the signal chain, although, as we shall see, considerable problems remain in employing such circuits in cost effective consumer products, especially as regards amplifiers.

SIGNAL SOURCES

The first digital consumer medium was not the compact disc;

rather, it was a sort of hybrid consisting of a videocassette deck and an outboard Sony PCM processor (Fig. 8-1). In this arrangement, the PCM processor is placed between the videocassette deck and an audio input—generally direct live feed from a microphone—and the audio signal is then recorded in digital form onto the sound track of the videotape. In playback, the process is reversed. The output from the VCR is routed through the PCM processor where it is converted back to analog, and that analog output is then fed into a line level input in a preamplifier. From then on, the analog signal is amplified in the usual manner.

Sony was the first manufacturer to market such a device, introducing its first consumer/semi-professional PCM processor back in 1977. The price then was approximately $4,000, and the unit was aimed at the serious recordist. Today, PCM processors are made by Aiwa, Nakamichi, Sansui, and Technics in addition to Sony, and prices go as low as $650. Although designated as consumer items, these units are more likely to be utilized by a professional musician or a movie sound man working on location. Few people are likely to buy them just for taping off the air, and there's next to no software for the format. (The tiny Direct-to-Tape recording label has issued a handful of classical titles.)

Sony Corporation, which has led in so many aspects of digital

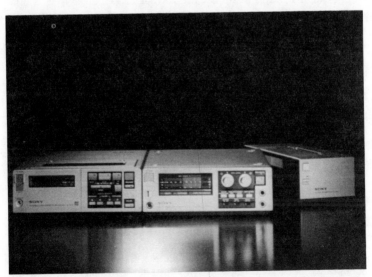

Fig. 8-1. Sony PCF-1 portable digital processor consisting of a Sony Betamax videocassette deck and a PCM processor. Machines of this type were the first digital sound sources offered to the public. Courtesy of Sony Corporation.

recording technology, is also pushing another digital tape format, 8 millimeter, which, in current stereo manifestation, carries an optional digital sound track and an analog video signal.

8 millimeter digital audio standards are significantly lower than those for the compact disc. The sampling frequency is only 31.5 kHz, and the resolution is 8 bit. Frequency range extends to less than 15 kHz, and while dynamic range is 90 dB, that figure is only achieved by virtue of a compander system similar to dbx. Inherent dynamic range is only 48 dB, less than that of an ordinary analog cassette.

The 8 mm digital audio sound track may be relatively low spec, but it does offer a great deal of recording time. In the low speed recording mode, a total of 24 hours of programming can be crammed into a single 8 mm cassette. No other home recording medium can match that.

The future of 8 mm as either an audio or a video medium seems unclear at this point. The medium is supported by Sony and Kodak, but little prerecorded software is yet available for it, and predictions that 8 mm will knock out VHS any time soon seem pretty dubious to me. The natural market niche for 8 mm appears to be as a highly portable replacement for the old 8 mm home movie camera. The digitized sound track offers no great benefits in terms of fidelity, and I fail to see what the format has to offer over a dbx equipped cassette deck for home audio recording.

Nevertheless, speculation is intense in the industry that 8 mm might, in time, become the universal tape medium for the home and replace the standard Philips analog cassette as well as the Beta and VHS video formats. In fact, such an eventuality could occur, not because 8 mm is superior in picture and sound quality to its rivals—it isn't—but because 8 mm lends itself to multiple applications. The 8 mm tape housing is smaller than that of a standard Philips cassette and, thus, 8 mm tapes can easily be utilized in portable applications such as personal stereos and automotive decks, or lightweight video camcorders. The universality factor is, itself, important because retailers strongly favor single formats. That is because single formats mean single inventories and less bookkeeping; they also mean less customer confusion. It is generally believed by industry analysts that the demise of quadraphonic sound was directly attributable to the multiplicity of formats, and that the slow acceptance of the videocassette medium in the 1970s resulted from the Beta-VHS rivalry. Japanese industry leaders know the desire of merchants for one format, and most such leaders agree in theory with the one format ideal.

Nevertheless, the Japanese consumer electronics industry has split over formats several times in the past in spite of its penchant for central planning. One company will spearhead the development of a new format and sink millions of dollars into research and development and, naturally, that company seeks a return on investment. All this is by way of saying that 8 mm is not unchallenged as the compact digital audio tape format and that as of this writing two serious rivals are waiting in the wings.

The first of these is known as rotary head digital audio tape (R-DAT). The basic technology is similar to that employed in the 8 mm format and in VHS and Beta. The pickup head, which reads the patterns of magnetization on the tape, is carried on a rotating drum that moves the head past the tape at a very high rate of speed and gives the effect of increasing tape speed to over 100 inches per second. High tape speed permits extended high frequency response, and the high "writing speed" produced by a rotating head simulates the effect of high tape speed in this respect. The end result is that the slow speed tape will accommodate the bandwidth needed for digital recording.

8 millimeters is, itself, a rotary head format. That may seem a little confusing, but R-DAT is an audio-only medium whereas 8 mm has a video track; and most significantly for our discussion, R-DAT has superior performance specifications—superior even to those of the compact disc format.

The Japan Electronic Industries Association announced standards for R-DAT late in 1985. Sampling frequency is 48 kHz instead of 44.1 kHz as with the compact disc, and resolution is a full 16 bits. Maximum program time per tape is one hour-30 minutes per tape side. Writing speed is approximately 120 inches per second, and the tape housing is a little over half the size of a standard Philips audio cassette. Incidentally, the higher sampling rate is employed primarily to prevent direct digital transfers from compact disc. Compact discs can still be copied, but the process involves a conversion of the signal into the analog domain and then a reconversion back to digital. Industry leaders want taped copies to be inferior to compact discs to reduce the incentive for duplicating commercial releases.

It should be emphasized that while standards have been set for R-DAT, and prototype R-DAT decks have been shown at Japanese trade shows, no consumer products have been released in the format. Industry scuttlebutt suggests a product introduction sometime in 1987, but such predictions may be premature. Traditionally, new formats are first marketed in Japan one to two years prior to their introduction into the United States. R-DAT is still completely unavailable in Japan as of this writing, May 1986.

The tardiness of the Japanese in introducing R-DAT is entirely understandable. The Japanese consumer electronics industry has an enormous stake in the success of the compact disc category and that success can only be complete if the public is not confused by multiple formats as happened with quad and home videocassette. The consensus in the Japanese consumer electronics industry is to hold off on R-DAT until the compact disc supplants the phonograph record, and only then introduce it as a replacement to the cassette format.

The problem with this approach is that in one application at least, DAT is difficult to segregate within its own little niche. That application is automotive audio where DAT can be easily adapted to an in-dash configuration and where it would appear to offer direct competition to the compact disc. The situation is made more complicated by the fact that several major manufacturers of automotive audio components clearly favor DAT over the compact disc as the medium of choice in the car. I cannot predict the resolution of this particular format conflict, but I suspect that DAT will, in fact, surface in the car within a couple of years and may retard acceptance of the automotive compact disc player.

Essentially, the same situation is obtained in the portable audio category. Portable handheld compact disc players are already available, but due to the dimensions of the disc itself, they are inherently more cumbersome than would be portables using a DAT format. But in the portable category the standard cassette is likely to remain the dominant format for many years to come simply because of the price sensitivity of portable components. Digital circuitry, laser tracking and rotary heads are costly compared to the heads, and transport, and bias circuits for analog cassettes, and consumers seem to want low cost in portables over high fidelity.

Yet another digital audio tape format exists in prototype—one known as stationary head digital audio tape, or S-DAT. S-DAT uses a fixed head like an ordinary cassette deck and a similarly slow tape speed—1-7/8 inches per second. Ordinarily this kind of speed would provide a bandwidth of at most 25 kHz, but S-DAT increases the information density and thus the bandwidth of the 1/8 inch wide tape strip by a tactic first developed in the early 1950s for video tape, namely, dividing the tape into a multitude of parallel tracks and reading the tracks simultaneously.

Firm standards have not been set for S-DAT as of yet, but the same 48 kHz sampling rate and 16-bit resolution of R-DAT will probably be adopted. The proposed standard calls for a total of 22 parallel tracks on a 1/8 inch strip of tape and, thus, each track is only 0.0056 inches wide. The pickup head is actually an array of heads with 22 magnetic gaps each 0.3 microns wide and 65 microns long. Thin film technology would be used to create the heads along with an etching process similar to that used for large scale printed circuits.

Current manufacturing methods dictate a cost of several thousand dollars per head, so, in other words, S-DAT is not a feasable technology yet. However, industry insiders predict the development of low cost manufacturing techniques sometime before the end of the decade.

S-DAT may seem fraught with unwanted complexity but it offers a few advantages over R-DAT. First, it provides something approaching random access. The fixed head makes locating selections a speedier process than is the case with a rotary head scheme, though the difference is only a matter of seconds. Second, S-DAT permits off-tape monitoring, a process whereby the tape can be checked for drop outs, overloads, recording level, etc. Off-tape monitoring is a feature on many home cassette decks and is of interest to serious home recordists; it is virtually impossible with a rotary head system.

Unfortunately, S-DAT has one very significant drawback, namely, playing time. Current proposed standards dictate a maximum of 30 minutes per side or one hour total. That's critically restrictive for a home recording medium. Of course, longer tapes could be used, but that means a larger housing.

S-DAT enjoys the backing of the huge and powerful Mashusita Corporation that owns Panasonic, Technics, JVC, and several other consumer electronics firms. For this reason alone it stands a chance of emerging as a consumer format, but I tend to think that R-DAT's technological head start will decide the issue. The format that is first on the market is apt to sweep the field. R-DAT is ready to go now; S-DAT is only a possibility.

Meanwhile, research and development on the cassette format has virtually ceased and cassette deck sales have flattened out. Clearly, the time has come for some new recordable medium, however it needn't necessarily be tape at all.

Apart from tape, many other experimental recording media for digitized audio signals have been developed. Most such media will never see practical deployment, but they're worth reviewing because at least some of them may see commercial applications.

As well as magnetic tape, several other magnetic recording media have been proposed for use in audio recording—among them magnetic cards, floppy discs, and bubble memories. At least two of these proposed media have been shown in prototype.

Magnetic cards could be used in conjunction with a technique known as vertical recording. In this process the magnetic recording medium is magnetized vertically to a considerable depth, and not just along a thin surface layer. The actual magnetic substance is the same as is used in tape—powdered metal or metal oxides. The vertical recording process permits the magnetization of a similar number of particles at a slow recording speed as can be achieved at a very high recording speed with conventional magnetic recording techniques.

Vertical recording can be done with suitable tapes as well as on cards, but given the enormous information density that can be attained per a given surface area, a card type magnetic recording blank is eminently practical.

Unfortunately, vertical recording entails an as yet very expensive head technology. The recording and playback systems shown thus far utilize two precisely aligned recording heads—one positioned above the blank and the other below. The magnetic fields from the two heads polarize a vertical cross-section of the blank. The heads themselves are made to very high tolerances and consist of a laminate of glass and metal. Sony has been experimenting with a single head vertical recording system, but that, too, will entail a very expensive head configuration.

Computer floppy discs have also been used to record digital audio sound tracks. A California based firm called Compusonics developed a proprietary technique for compressing digitized data that would give recording capabilities to the floppy discs that would approach those of the standard compact disc in spite of the inherently very limited storage capacities of floppies. The Compusonics system has been demonstrated at trade shows and may eventually see limited applications in semiprofessional recording, but given the already widespread use of VCRs in conjunction with PCM processors, and the eminent arrival of cheap highly portable DAT machines promoted by Japanese industrial cartels, the prospects for the Compusonics system do not appear favorable.

Bubble memory recording appears more promising but as of

this writing there is no indication that any major consumer electronics is prepared to promote it in any consumer audio application. A bubble memory is storage medium made up of tiny cylinders of magnetic material suspended in a film that also has magnetic properties. The cylinders are the "bubbles" and they are capable of limited movement within the film. These bubbles can be polarized and arranged in varying densities to represent a digital code. Bubble memories have very high information densities relative to magnetic tape. Potentially, a tiny chip could store an album length musical recording, though current bubble technology does not permit such data densities. Bubble memories are especially appealing because they involve no moving parts—except for the bubbles—and, thus, no wear during playback, and because they hold information indefinitely without the necessity of a power supply—unlike a solid state memory, that is, a conventional microchip.

Unfortunately, bubble memories are very costly and have found such limited applications in industry that costs aren't likely to decline anytime soon. Maybe some day there will be a place for them in sound recording, but not in the near future.

With the exception of bubble memory, all magnetic recording media are subject to wear, deterioration, and dropouts, and to that extent are clearly inferior to optical media such as the compact disc. The advantage of magnetic media, of course, is their recording capabilities which, up until now, have not been replicated in a practical optical medium with consumer applications.

Nevertheless, recordable optical media have been under development for over a decade and various prototypes working on a number of different principles have been demonstrated at trade shows. Most of the major Japanese electronics companies are heavily involved in research on recordable optical discs and there are strong reasons to suppose that a recordable optical disc rather than a magnetic medium will become the consumer recording medium during the 1990s.

Discs, by their very nature, have certain fundamental advantages over tape formats, or almost any magnetic format for that matter. The first advantage, and it is a considerable one for the consumer, is instant access to selected program material. Because the whole recording surface of a disc is constantly exposed during playback, the pickup can be cued in to the desired selection in a matter of seconds. The second advantage—one we have discussed at length previously—is permanence. Optical recording media using the disc format are noncontact media with no friction or abrasion on the surface of the disc. A third advantage is negligable maintenance requirements. Magnetic recording media tend to require a lot of routine maintenance operations on playback equipment such as head cleaning, degaussing, and azimuth adjustment. Optical recording playback devices are essentially maintenance free.

Recordable optical disc formats, at least two of which are currently available in the industrial market, take two basic forms, Write-Once, also termed Direct-Read-after-Write, and Record-Erase, or simply erasable. The first refers to disc media which can be recorded by the user only once. The second refers to formats on which a message can be recorded, erased, and rerecorded any number of times.

From a consumer standpoint, a record-erase format is much more desirable, but the possibility exists that a write-once format will become the consumer standard simply to protect DAT. A lot will depend on when the Japan Electronics Industries Association sees fit to formulate standards for recordable discs and when, if ever, the major manufacturers agree to a standard and a single format. As you will see in a moment, several designs already exist for both write-once and record-erase discs, but the write-once designs are much closer to the point at which they could be incorporated in cost effective consumer products. Manufacturing costs for any of the record-erase designs are still unacceptably high and would necessitate retail prices for machines in the thousands of dollars and, in some cases, unit prices in the hundreds of dollars for the actual recording blanks. Advances in manufacturing techniques could alter this situation within two years or so, but ultimately the progress of DAT will have a great bearing on the short term future of recordable discs.

All of the more promising write-once designs use high powered recording lasers similar in basic principle to those used to cut the master for compact discs. The laser is modulated by the digitized audio signal, and in most systems it creates a series of plateaus and depressions in the recording layer either by burning holes in a thin metal or plastic film, partially melting and thus deforming the film, or raising bubbles or blisters. In one system, an absorptive layer of silver halide is used to heat a thin polymer film to the point at which hot spots melt away leaving a series of holes. Another very unusual proposed system uses a low power laser that crystalizes points in a metallic recording layer and changes its reflectivity. No actual pits are created, just a succession of matte and glossy patches.

Most of the proposed record-erase systems take one of two forms: crystalline to amorphous or magnetic-optical. A third technology involving physical deformations of the disc's surface actually predates the other two but seems less likely to be adopted as the standard at present.

The crystalline to amorphous technique we have already touched upon preceeding description of write-once systems. Very simply, a crystalline structure has different reflective properties than an amorphous material made up of the same elements. Judicious applications of heat can be used to accelerate the growth of crystals or, alternately, to break them down. Panasonic is currently a leader in this technology of recordable discs and for several years has marketed industrial machines based on the crystalline-amorphous technique for document storage. In the Panasonic system the recording layer is made up of a mixture of tellurium monoxide and tellurium dioxide. The disc in its current application is FM encoded and may be used to store either video images or an audio signal. In late 1984, a moving picture version of the disc recorder was introduced to the industrial market with a capability of storing 18 minutes of programming. Noise reduction of the dbx type is applied to the audio signal for superior dynamic range and signal to noise ratio.

The Panasonic system currently uses FM rather than digital encoding simply because FM permits a greater information density than digital. The medium itself certainly could accept a digitized audio signal. Panasonic industrial disc recorders sell for prices in the five figures, and according to company spokespersons, a cost-effective consumer application is a long way off.

Magnetic-optical systems are a bit more complicated. A recording layer of terbium and iron alloyed with gadolinium or bismuth is heated with a recording laser while at the same time a magnetic bias is applied to the surface. An alternative system uses gold compounds instead of terbium in the recording layer. The heat reduces the coercivity of the recording material and permits magnetic polarization to take place. In this scheme the laser carries the digitized audio signal and the magnetic bias is held to a constant value. The operation is quite distinct from conventional magnetic recording in which the bias itself is modulated by the audio signal.

The magnetic polarizations of the thin recording layer have the effect of altering the polarity of light passing through the layer. By directing a laser beam through the layer and receiving it via an optical sensor equipped to detect polarity changes, a series of on-off pulses can be generated equivalent to the alteration of light and dark produced by the pitted track on a compact disc.

A recorder using such a system is actually offered by Nakamichi Corporation for industrial uses. The device has 16-bit resolution and includes a PCM encoder and decoder. The cost when introduced in 1984 was approximately $80,000. With dollar devaluation, that price could increase significantly. The machine, that Nakamichi has promoted as a research tool for evaluating CD ROM software, is aimed at major computer software companies and no consumer applications are envisioned at this time (Fig. 8-2). An American firm named Verbatim is also doing work with magnetic-optical recordable discs, but Verbatim's system, unlike Nakamichi's, does not require rare materials and is, consequently, much more cost effective. 25 dollar recording blanks are feasible with present technology.

Any consumer version of a magnetic-optical system would, necessarily, be completely incompatible with the compact disc because changes in polarity, and not reflectivity are the basis for the recording process. Compatability is apt to be a problem even with systems in which reflectivity rather than polarity is the operant principle. The physical parameters of the compact disc are very rigidly defined and the discs are constructed so that the pits are almost entirely nonreflective. The compact disc laser optics work with very sharply defined contrasts that cannot be easily duplicated in a recordable medium.

The third type of record-erase disc, that which carries the sig-

Fig. 8-2. Nakamichi OMS-1000 recordable optical disc system. Not a consumer item, this machine works on magnetic-optical principles and is primarily intended for evaluating software for the CD-ROM. Courtesy of Nakamichi.

nal within a series of surface deformations on the disc, uses a thermoplastic recording layer that dimples in response to the heating effects of the recording laser. A reapplication of the laser—unmodulated by an audio signal—will erase the recording and the surface can then be used for further recording.

Such a system was demonstrated at the University of Toronto back in 1977, and subsequently Xerox and CBS laboratories used this principle to make experimental recordings. Sansui has shown prototype machines based on this principle at trade fairs in recent years, but has not suggested that a consumer application is in the offing.

Many engineers involved in digital audio feel that neither disc nor tape will be the ultimate digital recording medium. All media utilizing mechanical transports have inherent limitations, principally sensitivity to microphonics and problems in maintaining speed control. Purely electronic systems do not suffer from such constraints, and the concept of storing digitized musical information in a solid state memory akin to the IC ROMs used in computers is highly intriguing.

Digital audio signals can be stored in such a manner and indeed they are, in certain types of musical synthesizers. The problems with this approach at present are twofold. First of all, solid state memories are inferior in information density by many orders of magnitude to optical discs. The storage capacity of microchips has been steadily improving, and, perhaps, by the turn of the century if not sooner, solid state memories may offer a serious alternative to the compact disc, but they are no where near comparable now. At such time as they do gain parity in information density, one still may wonder whether the audio industry would be prepared to phase out the compact disc format after a lifespan of less than two decades.

In any case, a move toward another medium is not the only course of development that consumer digital audio might take. The nonrecordable compact disc itself may evolve considerably during the closing years of this century. Right now a number of Japanese companies are quietly conducting research on a higher resolution digital audio optical disc—one that would actually deliver the perfect sound promised from the new format from the onset.

As was discussed in Chapters 1 and 2, persistent criticisms have been leveled at the sound of digital recordings by a minority within the audio industry, chiefly in the ranks of the manufacturers producing expensive, limited production "high end" audio components.

Critics of "digital sound" usually cite a tendency toward harshness in the high frequencies, a loss of spatial perspective and ambience, a subtle loss of resolution, a failure to delineate clearly the different sections of the orchestra, and blurring of instrumental timbres. Assessing the validity of such criticisms is difficult. Rigorously controlled listening tests conducted by James Boyk of California Institute of Technology indicate that PCM digital processors do produce audible alterations in an analog audio signal, in other words, the output differs from input. Why these alterations might be produced has been the subject of much debate in the industry, but most critics of digital recording feel that the decision to utilize the lowest sampling rates possible has compromised both professional and consumer digital recording media.

The proposed revision of the compact disc medium would address this bandwidth limitation by increasing the sampling rate three or four times over. Since the industry standard for professional digital mastering on magnetic tape is only 48 kHz, we would assume that higher sampling rates might also be adopted for mastering; if they were not, a radical increase in sampling rate for disc recording would make little sense.

The revised optical audio disc would no longer be compact in its physical dimensions and disc diameter might be anywhere from 8 to 12 inches, or roughly the size of a video laser disc. That is because higher bandwidth means more information on the disc surface. Since information density is pretty close to maximum already, a bigger disc is required to permit higher sampling rates while retaining playing times in the one hour range. If such an audiophile wideband optical disc is ever introduced, it will probably occupy a market niche somewhat different from the compact disc and will coexist with it. Very likely, machines would be made that could play either.

But all this is highly speculative at this point. I have considerable doubts as to whether the Japan Electronics Industries Association will ever promulgate standards for a wideband disc. And even if the JEIA should do so, the record companies would still have to be enlisted because no new format can succeed without software. With the advent of the compact disc, the consumer has already been asked in effect to rebuild his record collection, and at prices that are considerably above the unit costs of the traditional phonograph record. Will that same consumer a few years hence be equally willing to begin phasing out his CD collection in favor of a new medium which, in turn, may be phased out itself within a few years?

No one can answer those questions with any certainty. One can simply observe that the audio industry has changed very fundamentally in the matter of formats since the Japanese assumed leadership from the Americans in the mid-1960s. American audio industry leaders were extremely conservative, stressing compatability of all new formats with preceeding formats. If America had maintained leadership, the compact disc, at least as we know it, would never have been developed. Japanese industry leaders seem less concerned with compatability and continuity, and their reign has been marked by a proliferation of orphan formats.

It should be noted that there are industry observers who feel that the whole concept of individually owned music software could become obsolete, and that in the future no digital consumer medium will exist. Instead, the listener will pay for a cable service whereby he can call up musical selections from a vast central electronic memory—a sort of library of music.

Such predictions are difficult to evaluate. The recording industry depends upon sales to collectors and will certainly attempt to stimulate such sales in the face of any movement in the direction of dial-a-tune. And certainly if such a scheme were to succeed, it would be bound to have enormous effects on the music industry in general. Possibly, music with limited audiences would be threatened with virtual extinction since cable naturally tends toward local monopoly and any company wishes to strive for maximum sales with top selling categories.

But, as indicated, any discussion of digital cable services is extremely conjectural at this point. Compact disc is inching its way toward becoming the dominant format and no one in the hardware or software industries wants to rock the boat until that happens. Even should compact disc be supplanted before the turn of the century—an unlikely eventuality in my view—the already very large installed base of players would oblige the recording companies to continue to issue recordings in the compact disc format well into the next century.

Before I leave the topic of digital audio recording media, mention should be made of a final existing digital audio consumer format, the Laserdisc with digital sound track. The Laserdisc, the audio-video precursor of the compact disc, was encountered in the first chapter of this work. As you may recall, the Laserdisc format initially utilized a stereo FM soundtrack. A CX noise reduction encoding system was added to later players to improve signal to noise ratios, and in 1984, Pioneer Artists introduced software carrying a digitized audio signal. At the same time, a combination compact disc-Laserdisc player, the Pioneer CLD-900 was brought out that could play conventional compact discs and Laserdiscs as well as the new digital Laserdiscs. Actually, these digital-audio Laserdiscs continue to carry the FM soundtrack as well as the digital so that they may be reproduced on older machines. The digital soundtrack is, itself, identical to that on an ordinary compact disc. Only the width of the disc itself is different—Laserdiscs coming in 12 inch and 8 inch sizes instead of the 4 3/4 inch diameter of the compact disc.

Currently, only a few machines on the market are capable of playing the new digital Laserdiscs. In addition to the Pioneer machines, Luxman markets a combination player, basically a modified CLD-900 (Fig. 8-3), and TEAC, Sansui, and NAD also sell Pioneer machines under their own brand names. Yamaha makes a couple of Laserdisc machines that will play digital Laserdiscs in either 12 inch or 8 inch sizes but that won't play compact discs. In the future the majority of Laserdiscs will probably have digital sound tracks, but whether the Laserdisc format will ever gain widespread acceptance remains to be seen.

It is worth noting that standard compact discs have sufficient unused storage capacity to be able to store a multitude of still pictures, and that a few compact disc players on the market have video ports for transmitting this still frame output to a television monitor. As yet, virtually no CD software with video content is available, although hardware manufacturers have speculated that still pictures might serve the function of liner notes for albums of record-

Fig. 8-3. Luxman Model D-408 Compact Disc Player/Laservision Player. This is a modified Pioneer CLD-900 with dual power supplies for analog and digital sections, and a duo-beta feedback system for analog circuits. Courtesy of Alpine-Luxman.

ings. It would appear to me that a natural application would be in the presentation of educational materials, but as yet the recording industry has shown absolutely no interest in releasing such materials.

DIGITAL BROADCASTING AND CABLE TRANSMISSION

Digitized audio signals can be broadcast via radio waves through the atmosphere or alternately carried by copper wire or fiber optics. At present, all such applications are experimental because the Federal Communications Commission has not approved any digital broadcast or cable standard and the hardware manufacturers have not introduced any receivers for decoding such transmissions. Because digital transmissions require several times the bandwidth of analog transmissions with the same decoded audio bandwidth, any wide spread adoption of digital transmission over frequency ranges currently occupied by AM and FM radio and broadcast television would vastly reduce the number of stations. Because few existing stations wish to go out of business, the pressure against adopting digital transmission would be exceedingly strong.

However, in the extremely high frequency bandwidths currently allocated to direct broadcast satellite (DBS) transmission, a 16-bit 48 kHz sampling rate digitally encoded signal could be accommodated. So far, DBS, as opposed to other lower frequency satellite broadcast systems, has not gained much acceptance in the United States, but if it succeeds, digital broadcasts could become a reality and would eliminate many of the reception problems inherent with analog signals.

Cable seems a far more promising avenue for digital transmissions than does broadcast; station to station digital cable transmissions have been done in England since the early 1970s. With the proposed Cable Digital Audio/Data Transmission System (CADA), a stereo signal could be sent in the passband occupied by one CATV cable television channel. Standards would be identical to those of the compact disc format—16-bit resolution and a 44.1 kHz sampling rate—although the proposed standard would also permit four channel audio transmission at 10-bit resolution and a 32 kHz sampling rate. Unfortunately, the use of a CATV channel for digital audio transmission would not permit simultaneous transmission of a conventional video signal. The digital transmission would be audio only.

Thus far, such a digital cable transmission system has not been adopted anywhere in the United States, and no consumer hardware is available for receiving such a transmission. At this point, CADA is only a theoretical possibility.

DIGITAL AMPLIFIERS AND SIGNAL PROCESSORS

Digital amplifiers and signal processors predate the compact disc by a good many years, and today digital signal processors are in common use in recording studios. Digital amplifiers are not yet widely employed in any audio application, but in the near future we may expect to see them appear more frequently as consumer items. A detailed description of either digital signal processors or digital amplifiers is beyond the scope of this book, but a brief account of their basic operating principles is in order along with some discussion of their advantages. Since digital amplifiers have had the greater impact on consumer audio, these will be discussed first.

The term digital amplifier is used rather loosely to refer to three different kinds of power amplifiers. The first of these is an amplifier employing pulse width modulation of the audio signal followed by a sort of digital-to-audio convertor to remove the carrier frequency. In pulse width modulation, an audio signal is converted into a series of square waves. A square wave, as you may remember, is a complex waveform consisting of a fundamental and an infinite series of odd order harmonics. On an oscilloscope a square wave actually appears rectangular.

A square wave is produced by instantaneously opening an electronic gate, keeping it open at a constant value for some duration, and then instantaneously closing it. A perfect square wave is a theoretical not an actual electrical phenomenon, but a good approximation of a square wave can be produced by transistors capable of switching on and off very quickly.

In a pulse-width modulation amplifier also called a class D amplifier the output transistors continually switch on and off at a predetermined frequency called a carrier frequency. This frequency corresponds in certain respects to the sampling frequency in Pulse Code Modulation systems. However, the correspondence is not exact, because in Pulse Width Modulation the carrier frequency must be many times higher than the highest audio frequency for good fidelity. The Nyquist limit—double the highest frequency sampled—is nowhere near adequate.

In pulse width modulation the audio signal does not become a digital number with some precise bit resolution. Instead, the audio signal modulates the carrier causing the square waves in the carrier to vary in width according to the strength of the audio signal. The string of pulses of varying widths corresponds to the varying intensities within the analog waveform at input. Naturally, as the square waves grow wider they take longer to pass through the circuit, but the carrier frequency does not change, the pulses merely become closer together.

Pulse width modulation is actually nearer to frequency modulation than to pulse code modulation, and the circuitry required for modulation and demodulation is a good deal simpler. At output the modulated signal is converted back into sine waves by simply sending the pulses through a low pass filter. The notches representing intervals between transistor turn on and turn off are too brief to pass through the filter and a smooth analog waveform emerges.

Pulse width modulation amplifiers were first developed in the middle 1960s and during the 1970s a few were actually marketed by such companies as Infinity Systems and Sony. No domestic digital amplifiers are available in the U.S., although at least two companies, Yamaha and Bose, make class D amplifiers for the car.

Pulse width modulation, because of the output filtering requirements, is rather expensive to implement and in the past, amplifiers using the scheme have offered less than perfect performance. Unless the carrier frequency is much higher than the audio bandwidth, spurious tones can appear at output, and a carrier of 100 kHz is considered barely adequate. 250 kHz is much more acceptable, and some engineers feel that a one megahertz carrier is necessary for optimal results.

Unfortunately, very few commercially available transistors are capable of switching at high power at such frequencies. Certainly, the power bipolars employed in this application in the 1970s did not lend themselves to such uses. Modern high power MOSFET devices are much better suited to high speed switching and may permit the development of really successful digital amps in the near future, although the design presents other problems notably in the design of the output filter and the feedback loop. As with CD players, complex analog filters are used to strip the carrier and unless the carrier is very high in frequency the filter must be very steep which engenders considerable phase shift. Then, too, filters for high power applications necessitate very expensive close tolerance components and tend to suffer from drifting electrical values over time. Because the filter is in series with the speaker load, highly capacitative or inductive speaker loads can change filter values and compromise the functioning of the system. The fact that no digital home amplifier has ever been successfully marketed testifies to the magnitude of the design problems.

So why bother? Mainly for two reasons. Digital amps are extremely efficient and require very low idling currents compared to analog amps. They're cheap to operate and they generate very little heat and, thus, can be mounted in confined spaces with poor ventilation. For the same reason, they can be made extremely small and lightweight because they require none of the heavy metal heat sinks used in analog amps to dissipate the heat created by high electrical idling currents. A 500 watt per channel digital amp weighing less than 20 pounds is entirely feasible. A conventional class AB analog amp of the same power will weigh in the neighborhood of 100 pounds at a minimum while by way of comparison a class A analog amp in the 100 watt per channel power range will weigh at least 90 pounds. Differences in power consumption are equally dramatic. The 500 watt per channel amplifier is likely to idle at over 100 watts continuously. The digital amp of the same power will draw at most a few watts at idle.

Nevertheless, in terms of sheer musical accuracy and freedom from distortion, digital amplifiers do not out-perform their analog counterparts. Digitizing the audio signal in a tape recording will result in dramatic improvements in a number of key specifications. Digital power amplification brings no such benefits. Distortion figures are not superior to those of well designed analog amplifiers, and no one has ever seriously claimed that digital amps have subjectively superior sound quality.

The second type of digital power amp is simply an analog amplifier with a computer type switching power supply. To be more explicit, the signal circuitry is entirely analog while the power supply uses an oscillator—generally a pulse width modulation switching circuit—to produce very high frequency alternating current. This alternating current is not a carrier signal and is in no way modulated by the input signal. Instead, the current is smoothed into direct current by means of a small transformer and small value filter capacitors in the same way that ordinary 60 cycle ac from the wall plug is transformed into direct current in a conventional power supply.

Switching supplies are much more efficient than conventional power supplies, generate less heat and require only relatively inexpensive lightweight transformers and capacitors, but they also create a lot of electrical noise and interference and require extensive shielding. Most audio engineers do not believe that switching power supplies have arrived at the point at which they are suitable for domestic high fidelity applications and at present only one commercially available amplifier uses a switching power supply, the Berning EA-2100. That unit—a fascinating mixture of old and new—also uses vacuum tubes in the signal path.

The third type of digital amp is, as yet, only experimental. It uses pulse code or pulse number modulation and amplifies current by adding bits to the digitized signal according to an algorithm. The problems in switching high currents at rates in the hundreds of kilohertz required by such a system are formidable and cannot be said to have been completely solved. The advantage of such systems, should they be perfected, would be high efficiency and an almost total absence of any kind of distortion.

Voltage amplification in the digital domain through pulse code modulation is possible as well, but here efficiency is less of an issue. More significant is the fact that changes in tonal balance may be effected without generating phase shift—a nearly impossible feat to accomplish within the analog domain. Some designers envision completely digital circuitry from signal source right up to the loudspeaker outputs of the power amplifier; but to implement such a scheme would require conversion of the data to a different encoding scheme at the interface between amplifier and preamplifier if pulse code modulation were used because it, and pulse width modulation are not compatible. If a pulse code modulation amplifier could be perfected, of course, the problem would be solved.

Signal Processors

It is in the area of signal processing that digital circuits really provide substantial benefits over their analog counterparts. Equalizers, electronic crossovers, delay lines, and surround sound matrices can be designed with digital circuitry; already in critical professional recording applications, digital signal processors are winning increasing acceptance.

Digital equalization can be achieved by logic circuits that analyze waveforms for the presence of certain frequencies and then add or subtract bits at those frequencies. The process is much more complicated than using analog electronic filters made up of capacitors, inductors, and resistors, but as we indicated earlier, digital circuits permit tonal adjustments with absolutely no phase shift and with none of the distortions that analog equalizers introduce either. Currently, no digital equalizers are available in the consumer realm but at least one manufacturer is developing such a device and surely others will follow.

So far a handful of consumer digital signal processors have actually been marketed at one time or another. ADS seems to have introduced the first, a digital delay line for creating the effect of reverberation with a pair of rear speakers. This product, which was introduced in 1978, was ahead of its time, and failed in the market, probably due to the massive antipathy the buying public had developed toward the superficially similar quadraphonic sound systems. Very recently, Sony introduced a digital surround sound module capable of decoding Dolby surround sound video tracks as well as the old SQ quadraphonic system that still occasionally crops up in records, CDs, and music videos. And, finally, Threshold Corporation is offering phase coherent digital electronic crossovers for both domestic and automotive uses. We might note in passing that Pioneer has introduced digital demodulating circuitry for FM tuners.

Digital audio circuitry offers almost limitless possibilities for sound enhancement and in the future we will undoubtedly see digital signal processors having no parallels in the analog realm. Already in professional audio, digital circuits have been developed that will synthesize the missing overtones on old bandwidth-limited recordings and such capabilities may appear in consumer products in the future.

Finally, we should mention that experiments have reportedly been performed by several Japanese audio corporations on digital loudspeakers in which the loudspeaker itself forms the D/A convertor. Apparently, arrays of driver elements are used to accept parallel inputs representing each of the 16-bits and the elements are differentially activated according to the value of each sample. No one in the industry argues that a consumer application is anywhere close at this time, but by keeping the signal in the digital domain up to the speaker level, the electrical characteristics of the amplifier could be more closely atuned to the drivers' mechanical characteristics then is possible in the analog domain.

But sound itself remains analog and no matter how far the digitization of audio might proceed, nothing can change that.

Index

Edited by Molly Jackel